MOLLY KEANE

Molly Keane is the acclaimed
Time After Time, Loving and Giving, and many other
novels. She has lived in Ireland for all of her long life.

Sally Phipps is the daughter of Molly Keane. She is a
freelance journalist, married, and lives near her mother
in Co. Cork.

MOLLY KEANE'S IRELAND

An Anthology compiled by
MOLLY KEANE AND SALLY PHIPPS

With illustrations by Bob O'Cathail

HarperCollins*Publishers*

HarperCollins*Publishers*
77–85 Fulham Palace Road,
Hammersmith, London W6 8JB

This paperback edition 1994
1 3 5 7 9 8 6 4 2

First published in Great Britain by
HarperCollins*Publishers* 1993

Illustrations by Bob O'Cathail

The Authors assert the moral right to
be identified as the authors of this work

ISBN 0 00 637672 X

Set in Linotron Meridien

Printed in Great Britain
by Scotprint Ltd., Musselburgh

To Phyllis

CONTENTS

INTRODUCTION

On every return to Ireland, the country that owns me, I have an adjustment to make in comparison with where I have been and what I have seen, and I question my contentment. For what do I see? Dark, bony fields circling hills of darker gorse (only briefly golden) as they climb their way towards hungry mountain ranges, or down towards dangerous coasts. There is no medium of comparison between this country and, say, the lush fields of Gloucestershire, where lovely manor houses squat in their valleys and great houses shelter from the vulgar behind their parklands. In Ireland, it is only seldom that a house of interest, or the ruin of such a house, invades the picture and then, often, the austere outlines repel easy understanding. Even an author as perceptive as Virginia Woolf derided their strictness – their rain-grey facings chilling her as much as their long, unheated corridors and sweeping staircases. She wrote to her sister after a visit to Elizabeth Bowen in 1935, '. . . Elizabeth's home was merely a great stone box, but full of Italian mantelpieces and decayed eighteenth-century furniture and carpets all in holes.'

Bowen's Court is now demolished. Sadly, Irish houses of architectural quality, interest and value have always been in danger of loss and death: once from political warfare; now from neglect. Sometimes the remnants of a stable-yard, a half-circle of elegant Georgian architecture, heartbreakingly unspoilt, fanlights over every loose-box door, will cling to the ruin of a house. Wild birds fly in and out through the windowless and doorless spaces to circle the linked drawing-rooms and morning-rooms where, less than a hundred years ago, aunts mended sheets with darns finer than *petit point*, unaware in their elderly innocence of the merry tales such sheets could tell. Grey tweed skirts from Donegal fell to their ankles, long and undisturbed as fluted pillars.

Such memories melt into the lost background of lives long gone, just as the strict grey houses seem to soften at the edges in the gentle air and dissolve into the smoky-blue mountains beyond, and the rocky coast is subdued by the evening light lying narrowly for miles along the cliff-top fields.

My life in Ireland has been a long love affair and like all love affairs, has been broken and distorted many times, and many times restored to the tip of estimation. Sometimes, after a night of wild storms and floods, I wake from a heavy doze to see gleaming sun on the farthest headlands and distant waves, silent as the spread of a gull's wings, breaking behind each other on the shining sea. It is a liquidly bright, scentless morning, all colour spread with a full wet brush. Such contrasts, as startling as they are swift, are peculiarly sustaining to the creative artist and, in a life-enhancing way, mirror the romance, poetry and drama which have been part of Irish life since the first Celts wandered westwards across Europe.

The landscape retains a mystical quality which is as powerful a source for writers today as it has always been. There is a deep sense of place in Irish writing. We find it in the earliest poems of the Celtic monks with their jewel-like perception of weather, bird-song and plants; in the Sligo imagery of W. B. Yeats; in the importance of the landscape around Bowen's Court to Elizabeth Bowen, and of the hunting country of Skibbereen to Somerville and Ross; in the link between Joyce and Dublin, and that of Seamus Heaney with the boglands of Derry.

Aosdana (meaning 'Ireland's Treasures') was a term that encompassed all the travelling musicians, poets and storytellers who found hospitality, feastings, and an audience at the scattered courts of the continually warring Gaelic and Celtic chieftains. The hunger for music and drama, as strong in the Irish as the flow of tears or the course of rivers, maintained a strange neutrality between dissident kinglets and the pre-Norman invaders, and later between them and Norman settlers. The *Aosdana* wandered freely across bogs, forests, mountains and islands, telling their tales, reciting poetry, singing, playing the harp and the pipes, recounting scandal from court to court, and perhaps match-making when Norman inter-married with

Gael. Courts and kings dared not refuse them hospitality, although they were sometimes boisterous and troublesome, because their satire was much feared. Perhaps such minstrels served as the *Private Eyes* of their time.

The Normans, like other invaders, gradually became more Irish than the Irish. They identified with the Gaelic culture to such a degree that the English became fearful and outlawed it. Things worsened under Elizabeth I, and at the beginning of the seventeenth century, the Catholic aristocracy began to flee to Europe. Their confiscated estates were transferred to Protestant landlords planted by the English. Remnants of once powerful families who had not gone into exile sometimes became peasants on their own lands. The Gaelic culture collapsed and went underground. This gave rise to the oral tradition, hidden masses celebrated out of doors, the long memory and political secret societies which plague us to this day.

The Reformation caused England to espouse policies which drove Ireland into a dangerous subversiveness – England knew that Ireland was the back-door to her European enemies. The banished Catholic earls plotted with France and Spain. The English, understandably nervy, lost their sense of fair play, and in times of danger frequently and cruelly over-reacted. History for the two countries was almost exactly converse. Cecil Woodham-Smith describes it thus: 'Freedom for Ireland meant Philip of Spain and the Inquisition in place of Elizabeth I, it meant James II, instead of William III, it even meant, since misery and oppression make strange bedfellows, the victory of Napoleon.'

The monasteries (the seats of learning) and the manuscripts were destroyed, but the oral tradition grew in importance. The language and the culture were proscribed, but they continued in secret and in metaphor. *Aosdana* were significant carriers of the tradition in their music and poetry. They kept Ireland's flame alive in the persona of a beautiful young girl, Kathleen Ni Houlihan or Dark Rosaleen. In 'The Rose' (1893), Yeats took up the theme:

> Know that I would accounted be
> True brother of a company
> That sang to sweeten Ireland's wrong . . .

The Irish sense of drama is deeply embued in the attitude to death. Funerals are extremely important in community life and, alas, in political life. The Blasket Islands' literature includes accounts of wakes which comprise days of drinking, music, pipe-smoking, tall tales and lively intrigue. Wild outpourings of grief combine with a wildly festive atmosphere. Even today, a death in the family means open house with whiskey, tea and delicious food constantly on offer to a stream of visitors. The occasion is full of complex feeling, a time of sorrow, and a time for a party.

It is also painfully clear that there have been too many needless deaths in Irish history; in the course of nature, mortality is an outrage to the life force. The rage against death is expressed in the Keen, which has had its impact on literature, notably on Synge in his plays, and in his powerful evocation of the Keen on Aran. Beckett was perhaps influenced in a subterranean way by the Keen.

There is also in Irish people a noble acceptance of death. Some of the famine writings demonstrate this. One finds it in Humphry O'Sullivan's moving account of his wife's death in his diary of 1845.

Intrigue is never far from centre-stage in Irish life; it courses like an injection of oxygen along Irish blood vessels to Irish brains, whether its subject be the dead and the dying, matchmaking, horse-trading, or any subterranean dealing. This tendency to intrigue, combined with its side-kick, the whispered aside, has been of great benefit to our literature, giving an oblique and fascinating intensity to Irish drama through Synge, O'Casey, Hugh Leonard and Brian Friel.

The Irish do not avoid emotion, they almost always welcome it. Whether it is of love or hate, grief, scathing contempt or implacable anger, an outward and visible expression is necessary to them. Ceremony comes as easily as breathing, and expense – whether on whiskey or mass cards – is never considered.

Intrigue and ceremony are no strangers to the history of the Roman Catholic church, and it is surely the dramatic appeal of its countless rituals that strengthens the influence of religion in Irish society. To the unbeliever, the emotional bloodletting of the confessional box is a stunning example, a remarkable set piece: to the devout, a taxing performance matched only by the beatific ease which follows it.

Today, confession is an occasional, rather than a customary practice. The sweetness of its catharsis is movingly, if ironically, evoked by Joyce in *Portrait of the Artist* when Stephen unburdens himself to a gentle priest after his foray into Night-town. Protestants are inclined to regard the absolution of the confessional with a mixture of suspicion and envy.

Many writers have had trouble with the priesthood in the past. The twentieth-century Church has censored and attempted to destroy certain works of literature as ruthlessly as the Penal Code had destroyed the monks' manuscripts. Joyce is the best-known example of an Irish writer in exile. His works were banned in Ireland long after he was acknowledged elsewhere as the foremost innovatory novelist of our times. O'Faolain, Frank O'Connor – the nearest thing we possess to Chekov – and Hubert Butler, all of whom stayed here, suffered from censorship laws.

This is the narrow-minded side of Irish religion. It has little to do with a spirituality which is deeply rooted in many people, and linked to the extraordinary Irish imagination and the Irish landscape. In Penal times, the aristocrats who did not fly, bartered their Catholicism for their lands, but the majority of the people remained constant. The mass continued to be celebrated secretly on altars of rock in river glens or on sea cliffs. There is one such mass rock near my home at Ardmore. Tucked into sheer cliffs, it seems that you almost have to step off the edge of the world to reach it. It is strangely hidden from land or sea; visible only to a seagull's eye or God's eye. A huge sheet of limestone edged with lichens and, at the appropriate season, with sea pink and rock-rose. I am told it is now a trysting place for lovers. However, when it comes to my inward eye, I see it in its previous incarnation, with bedraggled figures slowly gathering on the horizon and disappearing over the cliff-face to worship in this beautiful but dangerous place.

The landscape is littered with such things, mass rocks, Ogham stones, holy wells, grave chambers of kings. Anything once held sacred seems to retain a whispering life, a tiny place, much diluted in the rituals of ordinary people's lives. Holy wells and mass rocks in inaccessible locations are visited still, partly for the sake of an outing, partly for some deeper, more ancient motive. The visionary qualities of the poet are connected with this world, and in Celtic times, it was recognized to be so. The old Irish word for poet, *Fili*, means See-er.

Poems and prayers are intertwined in the monks' verses. We find in them a worship of God, a celebration of the natural world, rituals of everyday life and simple supplication to a heavenly King. (Like and unlike the unruly earthly kings surrounding them.)

In Ireland, still, the most practical domestic doings shelter behind the drama of supplication. My own cook never put her bread to bake without a prayer for its rising, and a leading jockey I knew showed no embarrassment in murmuring a prayer against his horses' girths before he got up for his race. Yeats, in an inspired metaphor, said that the Irishman's mind escapes out of daily circumstance 'like a bough held down by a weak hand.' This flight from the surface of life comes in many forms. A certain amount of belief in the power of wishes and curses remains with us to this day. Holy wells still have their veneration: a white stone taken out of a wishing well indicates that a wish will be granted – or perhaps an ill-wish. A gate is unopened for a hundred years because a widow's curse foretold the death of the heir, should its latch be lifted. And there are foxes that leave their coverts to circle and howl all night around the house when a member of a certain family lies dying. According to Mary Carberry in the fascinating *The Farm by Lough Gur*, primroses were tied to the cows' tails at May eve to prevent the fairies from stealing milk. Primroses are evidently an anathema to fairies, and if you sprinkle them across the doorstep, you are entirely safe from intrusion.

Perhaps the most durable of all *Aosdana*'s legacies is the drama pregnant in the spoken word, a word spoken in language of near mythical beauty. The texture of the language has been created by the tension between the English and Irish tongues over decades. The settlers brought a beautiful Elizabethan English (the English of Shakespeare and Cranmer), which combined with the literal translations of Irish idioms to produce the vibrant speech of Irish-English. Even now, after the language has been eroded by the Americanisms of television, it is still rich and many chambered, like a great house. People had continued to speak Irish long after the writing of it was forbidden. Because the Gaelic heritage missed out on the advent of printing, much was lost, but much was handed down orally. Gradually, the spoken Irish was eroded by English, until it too almost disappeared, except for certain pockets. When the people called themselves dispossessed, it was not just the land they referred to, but to countless poets, poems, stories and songs that have slipped past the net of the oral tradition.

The translation of Gaelic literature into written English, and its influence on the writers of the Irish Literary Renaissance (at the turn of the century and later) is well known. Lady Gregory, founder with W. B. Yeats and Edward Martin of the Abbey Theatre, was an ascendancy chatelaine and an Irish scholar. She collected folk-lore and wrote it up in the speech of the people who told it to her. When she translated the Celtic sagas, she used the living Irish-English of people who thought in Irish, the voice of her neighbours at Coole, on the edge of Galway and Clare. This dialect became known as Kiltartanese. She kept open house at Coole for writers. The eighteenth-century house has been destroyed, but a tree still stands in the garden where Shaw, Yeats, Synge, O'Casey and many other visitors carved their names. Lady Gregory was a powerful character, full of courage and reality. People came to work under Coole's kindly, slate roof. She was an encourager of genius, but also a stern disciplinarian who 'could keep a swallow to its first intent.'

She was not of the people, but she loved and respected the country people around her and took up the image of nationhood hidden in their culture. She fostered an Ireland which was feared and rejected by most members of her class.

In many ways that now seem undesirably divisive, language helped to maintain a class difference down the years. The settled ascendancy spoke English between themselves, into the days when English public schools emphasized the differences which helped to divide the classes and keep them socially apart. Only the beautiful languages of fox hunting, racing, shooting and fishing were shared and broke the silence between the classes in that great union of sport that is careless of politics and innocent of terrorism. We see this reflected in the writings of Trollope, and Somerville and Ross. In Ireland, the horse has ever been a bridge between the classes. 'The horse has always been the heroic solvent of Irish evils.' (V. S. Pritchett)

The heightened sense of drama in the Irish character is reflected in everyday speech. This dramatic, poetic and witty use of language in ordinary life is extraordinarily useful to writers. It is waiting to be picked up like shells on a beach. In the hands of a master, it is magic, but it is a heady brew and it can be mis-used. Profaners who take the froth from the top without understanding the complexity of the depths have brought us the imbecile aphorism of the comic Irishman, for example. The Irish are sardonic often, lyrical often, but comic – never.

Even Thackeray, whose *Irish Sketch Book* has many wonderful moments, offended occasionally, sometimes making use of the castle-to-pigsty, begorrah, top-of-the-morning style as farcical fodder to lighten journalism. Trollope was more restrained. His job as an inspector of post offices kept him here over a longer period and deepened his understanding, as did his knowledge of horses. The hunting field is an exhilarating place from which to observe the Irish at their very best. Later, when he became England's most popular novelist, Trollope said he 'wrote to hunt'.

It was not until the wartime 1940s, from which Ireland excluded herself, that her journalists took a sharp turn away from the comic Irish convention, and R. M. Smylie, literary editor of the *Irish Times*, gave room and space to two brilliant columnists whose writing cleared the horizon from the mist that does be on the bogs, substituting for it 'the plain people of Ireland' whose complaints against every aspect of Dublin life, political or domestic, were retailed for us through the mouth-piece of a serious character known only as 'the Brother'. The author of this new style, Miles nagCopaleen, (alias the novelist, Flann O'Brien) was a Celtic scholar who turned his back on the Book of Kells to illuminate with sharp wit and just disparagement, a middle-class life unknown to any audience unfamiliar with the Dublin pub life.

At the same time, the immortal Paddy Campbell lent his talent to the dissection of the Dublin literati who frequented his mother's salon in the Wicklow Hills. A little later, the fox hunting and racing establishment was to come under his lash and his perpetual enchantment.

It is impossible for anyone who loves Ireland, and loves words, to get away from Yeats. I make no apology for the fact that this preface is littered with quoted fragments of his vision, the crumbs from a rich man's table. It cannot be otherwise. The toughness, beauty and endurance of his word-smithing, and the sheer quality of his poems transcend easily his systems and notions, which are sometimes rather hard to swallow.

Of course, he does not get it right every time. He shed skins all of his life. Remarkably often, however, if one wishes to throw light on some aspect of what it means to be Irish – the struggle of it and the glory – the phrase is there, expressed more truly than anyone else can do it.

The idea of composing an anthology is a very seductive one. Indeed, it would be the greatest fun if one had a decade or a lifetime at one's disposal. In reality, one is haunted, almost from the start, by what is left out.

My daughter and I have worked together. Born as we are into the context of very diverse times, our views of Ireland sometimes overlap, but are full of shades of difference. This difference of view is useful, but it can still only reflect a fraction of Ireland's treasure.

It is our hope that you will find in these pages something of the myriad world that lies between Yeats' two extremes, that of the country where a man 'can be so battered, badgered and destroyed that he's a loveless man,' and the Ireland in which 'all things hang like a drop of dew upon a blade of grass.'

MOLLY KEANE
July 1993

Under the auspices of Mr Charles Haughey, the word *Aosdana* has been revived, and applied to an Irish Government institution which takes under its wing creative artists who have made a significant contribution to the visual arts, music and literature in Ireland. Before the new *Aosdana*, such artists pursued their lonely and often despairing ways in and out of galleries, concert halls and publishers' offices, the older among them often breathing their last in undignified circumstances. The revival of *Aosdana* brought encouragement to the young, and a blessed lull in the anxieties of the old.

I have long loved the paintings of Derek Hill, whose landscape 'The back of Tory Island' forms the jacket of this book.

His portraits became familiar to me first. They were such an invigorating change from the dull, efficient likenesses of the gentlemen of the Ascendency painted by Lawrence, Birly and others that I had grown up with. It struck me that these earlier portraits of strong upholders of the Protestant religion also showed (in many instances) the reputed rakes and rapers of their day, but, in all the pictures which still loom above chimney-pieces or paper the walls of dining-rooms, the artists do not allow a suggestion of louche goings-on.

Derek Hill's subjects extend across all of Irish life. In his portraits of the Ascendency he allows them their salty moments and the style and humour to accept life as it comes and goes and changes. In a side-long dimple prettiness is not avoided, neither (where it occurs) is a suspicion of the louche. Certain portraits go further in their revelations than any writer might probe. In a well-behaved aesthetic face, one perceives a quiet threat about the lips shut on some secret. Was there a hurt in love? Was there a betrayal? If so, it was not forgiven.

Derek's landscapes are painted in the same manner in which his portraits of the Ascendency allow for sultry moments. The smell of a dark cottage is behind a dwarfish geranium leaning into the mean sunlight which comes through a small-paned window. He observes and transforms the sea's spite and anger to follow it to his masterpiece, *A Quiet Wave* – the whole of an evening in its placidity.

M. K.

ANTHOLOGIES

I open an anthology with some apprehension always that my mind will be confused ... Anthologies too often are like museums and picture galleries, where works conceived in the most varied moods are set side by side. I find it difficult to change my mood passing from picture to picture. If I look at too many the effect is to stupefy.

Æ, The Living Torch

THE UNDYING TONGUE

THE SCHOLAR'S LIFE

Sweet is the scholar's life,
  busy about his studies,
the sweetest lot in Ireland
  as all of you know well.

No king or prince to rule him   5
  nor lord however mighty,
no rent to the chapterhouse,
  no drudging, no dawn-rising.

Dawn-rising or shepherding
  never required of him,   10
no need to take his turn
  as watchman in the night.

He spends a while at chess,
  and a while with the pleasant harp
and a further while wooing   15
  and winning lovely women.

His horse-team hale and hearty
  at the first coming of Spring;
the harrow for his team
  is a fistful of pens.   20

THOMAS KINSELLA, *Poems of the Dispossessed*

IMAGES OF THE PAST

It is not the literal past, the 'facts' of history, that shape us,
but images of the past embodied in language ... we must
never cease renewing those images; because once we do, we
fossilize.

BRIAN FRIEL, *Translations*

3

LANGUAGE

The Gaelic is, as I have said, a language without a modern literature, but it is a language of prodigious diversity of sound and expressiveness of phrase. Owing to its peculiar anatomy of 'broad,' 'slender,' 'aspirated' and 'eclipsed' consonants, it has about twice the number of sounds that other European languages can boast; sounds, too, for most of which there are no precise equivalents in any other tongue. (For instance: d broad is dth, d slender is dy, d aspirate broad is a sort of gargle, d aspirate slender is almost y, d eclipsed broad is an n with clenched teeth, d eclipsed slender is ny. There is no d as we know it in English, French, German etc.; and so with the other consonants.) The softening and eclipsing of initial consonants (according to complicated and uncertain rules) cause the words to dissolve and change their shapes like objects in a mist; more than with most languages, the student has to speak and think in unit-sentences rather than unit-words, as it were single indivisible spasms of feeling or imagination; 'the colours run' on the palette – or the palate – so that he is lost if he has not a fine ear and a mobile larynx. As for the expressiveness of the Gaelic folk-idiom, only the 'Irish English' of Synge's plays can give strangers some idea of it; it is the language, if not of a race of poets (perhaps we are too poetical to be poets, as Wilde said), then at least of a race which has 'tired the sun with talking,' a language of quips, hyperboles, cajoleries, lamentations, blessings, curses, endearments, tirades – and all very often in the same breath; but not a language into which you could easily translate, say, the *Encyclopaedia Britannica*.

ARLAND USSHER, *The Face and Mind of Ireland*

CUSTODIANS OF THE LANGUAGE

It is indeed a distinction of the educated Irish – whatever their class or derivation – that they give back to English its modulated beauty without fashionable or vulgar distortions – and of the uneducated that they give it vehemence and colour. This has made them masters of English rhetoric and prose and, with the Welsh, custodians of the language.

V. S. PRITCHETT, *At Home and Abroad*

CAROLAN

Of all the bards this country ever produced, the last and the greatest was Carolan the Blind. He was at once a poet, a musician, a composer, and sung his own verses to his harp. The original natives never mention his name without rapture; both his poetry and the music they have by heart; and even some of the English themselves, who have been transplanted there, find his music extremely pleasing. A song beginning 'O Rourke's noble fare will ne'er be forgot,' transplanted by Dean Swift, is of his composition; which, though perhaps by this means the best known of his pieces, is yet by no means the most deserving. His songs, in general, may be compared to those of Pindar, as they have frequently the same flights of imagination, and are composed (I don't say written, for he could not write) merely to flatter some man of fortune upon some excellence of the same kind. In these one man is praised for the excellence of his stable (as in Pindar), another for his hospitality, and a third for the beauty of his wife and children, and a fourth for the antiquity of his family. Whenever any of the original natives of distinction were assembled at feasting or revelling, Carolan was generally there, where he was always ready with his harp to celebrate their praises. He seemed by nature formed for his profession; for as he was born blind, so also he was possessed of a most astonishing memory, and a facetious turn of thinking, which gave his entertainers infinite satisfaction. Being once at the house of an Irish nobleman, where there was a musician present who was eminent in the profession, Carolan immediately challenged him to a trial of skill. To carry the jest forward, his lordship persuaded the musician to accept the challenge, and he accordingly played over on his fiddle the fifth concerto of Vivaldi. Carolan, immediately taking his harp, played over the whole piece after him, without missing a note, though he had never heard it before; which produced some surprise: but their astonishment increased when he assured them he could make a concerto in the same taste himself, which he instantly composed, and that with such spirit and elegance that it may compare (for we have it still) with the finest compositions of Italy.

OLIVER GOLDSMITH, *Prose Works*

The *Aisling* is lyric poetry at its most lyrical . . . Though not the folk-poetry of the period, they were the popular songs of the period: they passed quickly from mouth to mouth, were hankered after, were stored in the brain, were given down from father to son. In the summer of 1915, in Kerry, about two miles from Dingle, I heard an old illiterate woman break suddenly into one of them, changing, however, not without a twinkle in her eye, a word here, a name there, to make the poem fit in with the fortunes of the Great War in its early phase. In the Munster of the eighteenth century, there can scarcely have been a single peasant's hut which did not shelter beneath its thatch either such an old woman as this, or an old man of like temper – Gaels who would have thousands upon thousands of lines of well-wrought verse laid up within their memories. Illiterates, yet learned in literature, they were critics who appraised the poems as was right, that is, as lyric poetry, and not as anything else. They gave them welcome rather for the art that was in them than for the tidings. One such poem they put against another, testing both, comparing this poet's opening with that other's; or matching this description (always elaborate) of the flowing locks of the *Spéir-bhean* (the Vision) with that other's painting of them, or evaluating this song's close by the aid of the remembered cadences of a hundred others.

DANIEL CORKERY, *Hidden Ireland*

THE HIGH POETS ARE GONE
For the family of Cúchonnacht Ó Dálaigh

The high poets are gone
    and I mourn for the world's waning,
the sons of those learned masters
    emptied of sharp response.

I mourn for their fading books   5
    reams of no earnest stupidity,
lost – unjustly abandoned –
    begotten by drinkers of wisdom.

After those poets, for whom art and knowledge were
    wealth,
  alas to have lived to see this fate befall us: 10
their books in corners greying into nothing
  and their sons without one syllable of their secret
    treasure.

THOMAS KINSELLA, *Poems of the Dispossessed*

Like Jack Yeats and other artists and writers, Æ gave
'Evenings'. His weakness, I was told, was very typical of all of
us . . . he talked, particularly during the latter years of his life.
This was particularly objected to by those who wished to talk
unceasingly themselves. My mother tells me of Æ's boom once
being minced and disintegrated by the cheerful clip-clip of
the English historian Rowse's stultifying Oxford comments.
Personally, on my one evening there, I loved hearing the poet
talk, though I do wish he had hit on any subject for eulogy
rather than American skyscrapers. But that again is so like
Dubliners: Joyce is said to have talked ceaselessly about potato
crops to those who called on him in Paris. Shaw, my mother
told me, had been disillusioningly replenished with anecdotes
about himself. Only Synge, greatest word-spinner of all in writing, had been a silent man.

OLIVIA ROBERTSON, *Dublin Phoenix*

THE IRISH STORYTELLER

His mind constantly escaped out of daily circumstance, as a
bough that has been held down by a weak hand suddenly
straightens itself out.

W. B. YEATS, from the introduction to Lady Gregory's
Cuchulain

There are only two dialects of Irish, plain Irish and toothless Irish, and lacking a proper acquaintance with the latter, I think I missed the cream of the Tailor's talk, though his English was very colourful and characteristic. But I noticed how almost every phrase he spoke was rounded off by an apt allusion. When Anstey hurried, the old man, enthroned on his butter-box by the fire, reproved her and instantly followed up with the story of the Gárlach Coileánach's mother. 'A year is past since my mother was lost; she'd be round the lake since then.' Or when someone spoke of a girl having a baby he came back with: 'She's having last year's laugh's cry.' In Irish, poems, rhymes and proverbs tumbled from him literally in hundreds.

FRANK O'CONNOR, *Munster, Leinster and Connaught*

It is a pleasure to be with him, especially when one meets him for the purpose of literary discussion; he is a real man of letters, with an intelligence as keen as a knife, and a knife was required to cut the knots into which Edward had tied his play, for very few could be loosened. The only fault I found with Yeats in this collaboration was the wariness into which he sank suddenly, saying that after a couple of hours he felt a little faint, and would require half an hour's rest.

We returned to the play after lunch, and continued until nearly seven o'clock, too long a day for Yeats, who was not so strong then as he is now, and Lady Gregory wrote to me, saying that I must be careful not to overwork him, and that it would be well not to let him go more than two hours without food – a glass of milk, or, better still, a cup of beef-tea in the afternoon, and half an hour after lunch he was to have a glass of sherry and a biscuit. These refreshments were brought up by Gantley, Edward's octogenarian butler, and every time I heard his foot upon the stairs I offered up a little prayer that Edward was away in his tower, for, of course, I realised that the tray would bring home to him in a very real and cruel way the fact that his play was being changed and rewritten under his very roof, and that he was providing sherry and biscuits in order to enable Yeats to strike out, or, worse still, to rewrite his favourite passages. It was very pathetic; and while pitying and admiring Edward for his altruism, I could not help thinking of two children threading a bluebottle. True that the bluebottle's plight is worse than Edward's, for the insect does not know why it is being experimented upon, but Edward knew he was sacrificing himself for his country, and the idea of sacrifice begets a greater exaltation of mind, is in fact, a sort of anaesthetic; and sustained by this belief we, Yeats and I, worked on through the day, Yeats tarrying as late as seven o'clock in order to finish a scene, Edward asking him to stay to dinner, a kindness that proved our undoing, for we lacked tact, discussing before Edward the alterations we were going to make. He sat immersed in deep gloom, saying he did not like our adaptation of the first act, and when we told him the alterations we were going to make in the second, he said:

But you surely aren't going to alter that? Why do you do this? Good heavens! I wouldn't advise you.

GEORGE MOORE, *Hail and Farewell*

COOLE PARK, 1929

I meditate upon a swallow's flight,
Upon an aged woman and her house,
A sycamore and lime-tree lost in night
Although that western cloud is luminous,
Great works constructed there in nature's spite
For scholars and for poets after us,
Thoughts long knitted into a single thought,
A dance-like glory that those walls begot.

There Hyde before he had beaten into prose
That noble blade the Muses buckled on,
There one that ruffled in a manly pose
For all his timid heart, there that slow man,
That meditative man, John Synge, and those
Impetuous men, Shawe-Taylor and Hugh Lane,
Found pride established in humility,
A scene well set and excellent company.

9

They came like swallows and like swallows went,
And yet a woman's powerful character
Could keep a swallow to its first intent;
And half a dozen in formation there,
That seemed to whirl upon a compass-point,
Found certainty upon the dreaming air,
The intellectual sweetness of those lines
That cut through time or cross it withershins.

Here, traveller, scholar, poet, take your stand
When all those rooms and passages are gone,
When nettles wave upon a shapeless mound
And saplings root among the broken stone,
And dedicate – eyes bent upon the ground,
Back turned upon the brightness of the sun
And all the sensuality of the shade –
A moment's memory to that laurelled head.

W. B. YEATS, *Collected Poems*

THE READING LESSON

Fourteen years old, learning the alphabet,
He finds letters harder to catch than hares
Without a greyhound. Can't I give him a dog
To track them down, or put them in a cage?
He's caught in a trap, until I let him go,
Pinioned by 'Don't you want to learn to read?'
'I'll be the same man whatever I do.'

He looks at a page as a mule balks at a gap
From which a goat may hobble out and bleat.
His eyes jink from a sentence like flushed snipe
Escaping shot. A sharp word, and he'll mooch
Back to his piebald mare and bantam cock.
Our purpose is as tricky to retrieve
As mercury from a smashed thermometer.

'I'll not read any more.' Should I give up?
His hands, long-fingered as a Celtic scribe's,
Will grow callous, gathering sticks or scrap;
Exploring pockets of the horny drunk
Loiterers at the fairs, giving them lice.
A neighbour chuckles. 'You can never tame
The wild-duck: when his wings grow, he'll fly off.'

If books resembled roads, he'd quickly read:
But they're small farms to him, fenced by the page,
Ploughed into lines, with letters drilled like oats:
A field of tasks he'll always be outside.
If words were bank-notes, he would filch a wad;
If they were pheasants, they'd be in his pot
For breakfast, or if wrens he'd make them king.

RICHARD MURPHY, *High Island*

THE GIVEN NOTE

On the most westerly Blasket
In a dry-stone hut
He got this air out of the night.

Strange noises were heard
By others who followed, bits of a tune
Coming in on loud weather

Though nothing like melody.
He blamed their fingers and ear
As unpractised, their fiddling easy

For he had gone alone into the island
And brought back the whole thing.
The house throbbed like his full violin.

So whether he calls it spirit music
Or not, I don't care. He took it
Out of wind off mid-Atlantic.

Still he maintains, from nowhere.
It comes off the bow gravely,
Rephrases itself into the air.

SEAMUS HEANEY, *Selected Poems*

I AM RAFTERY

I am Raftery the poet,
  Full of hope and love,
With eyes that have no light,
  With gentleness that has no misery.

Going west upon my pilgrimage
  By the light of my heart,
Feeble and tired,
  To the end of my road.

Behold me now,
  And my face to a wall,
A-playing music,
  Unto empty pockets.

DOUGLAS HYDE (Trans.), *Studies and Translations from the Irish*

QUATRAIN
For Robert Óg Carrún

Blessings on your head in a glowing heap for ever,
beloved, as you grip the great wooden carrying-harp.
With a stream of polished playing, profound and sweet,
you have banished the spiders' webs out of all our ears.

THOMAS KINSELLA, *Poems of the Dispossessed*

ARAN ISLANDS

On the low sheets of rock to the east I can see a number of
red and grey figures hurrying about their work. The continual
passing in this island between the misery of last night and the

splendour of today, seems to create an affinity between the moods of these people and the moods of varying rapture and dismay that are frequent in artists, and in certain forms of alienation. Yet it is only in the intonation of a few sentences or some old fragment of melody that I catch the real spirit of the island, for in general the men sit together and talk with endless iteration of the tides and fish, and of the price of kelp in Connemara.

J. M. SYNGE, Aran Islands

LIGHT DYING

*In Memoriam Frank O'Connor (Michael
O'Donovan)*

Climbing the last steps to your house, I knew
That I would find you in your chair,
Watching the light die along the canal,
Recalling the glad creators, all
Who'd played a part in the miracle;
A silver-haired remembering king, superb there
In dying light, all ghosts being at your beck and call,
You made them speak as only you could do

Of generosity or loneliness or love
Because, you said, all men are voices, heard
In the pure air of the imagination.
I hear you now, your rich voice deep and kind,
Rescuing a poem from time, bringing to mind
Lost centuries with a summoning word,
Lavishing on us who need much more of
What you gave, glimpses of heroic vision.

So you were angry at the pulling down
Of what recalled a finer age; you tried
To show how certain things destroyed, ignored,
Neglected was a crime against the past,
Impoverished the present. Some midland town
Attracted you, you stood in the waste

Places of an old church and, profoundly stirred,
Pondered how you could save what time had sorely
    tried,

Or else you cried in rage against the force
That would reduce to barren silence all
Who would articulate dark Ireland's soul;
You knew the evil of the pious curse,
The hearts that make God pitifully small
Until He seems the God of little fear
And not the God that you desired at all;
And yet you had the heart to do and dare.

I see you standing at your window,
Lifting a glass, watching the dying light
Along the quiet canal bank come and go
Until the time has come to say good-night:
You see me to the door; you lift a hand
Half-shyly, awkwardly, while I remark
Your soul's fine courtesy, my friend, and
Walk outside, alone, suddenly in the dark.

But in the dark or no, I realise
Your life's transcendent dignity,
A thing more wonderful than April skies
Emerging in compelling majesty,
Leaving mad March behind and making bloom
Each flower outstripping every weed and thorn;
Life rises from the crowded clay of doom,
Light dying promises the light re-born.

BRENDAN KENNELLY, *A Time for Voices*

THE INCOMPARABLE SKILL OF THE PEOPLE IN MUSICAL INSTRUMENTS

It is only in the case of musical instruments that I find any commendable diligence in the people. They seem to me to be incomparably more skilled in these than any other people that I have seen.

The movement is not, as in the British instrument to which we are accustomed, slow and easy, but rather quick and lively, while at the same time the melody is sweet and pleasant. It is remarkable how, in spite of the great speed of the fingers, the musical proportion is maintained. The melody is kept perfect and full with unimpaired art through everything – through quivering measures and the involved use of several instruments – with a rapidity that charms, a rhythmic pattern that is varied, and a concord achieved through elements discordant. They harmonize at intervals of the octave and the fifth, but they always begin with B flat and with B flat end, so that everything may be rounded with the sweetness of charming sonority. They glide so subtly from one mode to another, and the grace notes so freely sport with such abandon and bewitching charm around the steady tone of the heavier sound, that the perfection of their art seems to lie in their concealing it, as if 'it were the better for being hidden. An art revealed brings shame.'

GIRALDUS CAMBRENSIS, *History and Topography of Ireland* (Trans. John O'Meara)

IRISH PLASTERWORK

The wall decoration wins attention as much for its spirited execution of detail as for its order and apparent spontaneity. Its freedom exhibits almost all the elements of early and mid-century ornament: interlaces of flat or foliated ribbon strapwork; shell and palmette, acanthus and flamboyant palms, lion-masks with manes deriving from Louis XIV sun-rays; musical trophies: horns, trumpets, violins and songbooks; flowers swinging in garlands and bouquets, birds in lively action or, as on the coving, half stylised. This lucid decoration is ordered in charming framework which plays a part of its own in the general scheme, and is lit by a Venetian window – its capital, soffits and entablature fully enriched. The work is carried past the window on two panels with more musical trophies, violins and a songbook, to the landing which is more formally decorated with panels of interlaces and vine-leaf swags like those in the parlour below.

ROBERT WEST, '86 St Stephens Green 1752' (in *Dublin Decorative Plasterwork*, ed. C. D. Curran)

GLASS

... His shop is now completely stored
With choicest glass from Waterford –
Decanters, Rummers, Drams and Masons,
Flutes, Hob Nobs, Crofts and Finger Basons,
Proof bottles, Goblets, Cans and Wines,
Punch Juggs, Liqueurs and Gardevins;
Salts, Mustards, Salads, Butter Keelers,
And all that's sold by other dealers,
Engraved or cut in newest taste,
Or plain – whichever pleases best;
Lustres repaired or polished bright,
And broken glasses matched at sight;
Hall globes of every size and shape,
Or old ones hung and mounted cheap.

Trade Circular 1790 from Marsden Haddock of Cork (*Cork Archaeological Journal* 1901) in *Irish Glass*, DUDLEY WESTROP, revised and edited
by Mary Boydell

THE ANTECEDENTS OF HISTORY

I have a quarrel with historians, for they seem to assume that
the birth of great imaginations is not subject-matter for history
as much as great wars, or treaties or political or economic
systems! Is history only to deal with effects, and not with
causes? Great wars are the result of conflicting imaginations,
which are anterior to wars as causes precede effects. Treaties
are the equilibrium established after the imaginative storm has
worn itself out. Economic and political systems represent more
or less fixed or solid states of soul in a civilisation; but once
they had their fiery and volatile states in the imagination of
humanity. The true history of Ireland would attach as much
importance to the creation of bodiless moods as to material
events, and be as concerned with literature as with laws, con-
flicts, warriors or statesmen. What is a nation but an imagination common to millions of people? Is there anything else to
it? I doubt it. Race does not make nationality, for nearly all
the greatest nations are composite. Natural boundaries are not
a justification for independent states. There are mountains and

rivers inside states which might equally split them up as the rivers or mountains on their borders. Religions are no mark of nationality, for they are international.

Æ, *The Living Torch*

The demesne of Edgeworthstown is judiciously and abundantly planted; and the dwelling-house is large and commodious. We drove up the avenue at evening. It was cheering to see the lights sparkle through the windows, and to feel the cold nose of the house-dog thrust into our hands as an earnest of welcome; it was pleasant to receive the warm greeting of Mrs Edgeworth; and it was a high privilege to meet Miss Edgeworth in the library – the very room in which had been written the immortal works that redeemed a character for Ireland and have so largely promoted the truest welfare of human-kind. We had not seen her for some years – except for a few brief moments – and rejoiced to find her in nothing changed; her voice as light and happy, her laughter as full of gentle mirth, her eyes as bright and truthful, and her countenance as expressive of goodness and loving-kindness, as they had ever been.

The library at Edgeworthstown is by no means the reserved and solitary room that libraries are in general. It is large, and spacious, and lofty; well stored with books, and embellished with those most valuable of all classes of prints – the suggestive; it is also picturesque – having been added to so as to increase its breadth – the addition is supported by square pillars, and the beautiful lawn seen through the windows, embellished and varied by clumps of trees, judiciously planted, imparts much cheerfulness to the exterior. An oblong table in the centre is a sort of rallying-point for the family, who group around it – reading, writing, or working; while Miss Edgeworth, only anxious upon one point, – that all in the house should do exactly as they like without reference to her, sits quietly and abstractedly in her own peculiar corner, on the sofa; her desk, upon which lies Sir Walter Scott's pen, given to her by him when in Ireland, placed before her upon a little, quaint table, as unassuming as possible.

Visit of Mr and Mrs Hall to Maria Edgeworth, *Ireland: Scenery and Character 1825–40*

Stretching himself on the old stretcher-bed by the wall that separated his room from the hall outside, Sean halted his mind from thinking out the new play he intended to write. The Abbey Theatre had accepted one, after long consideration, and he had reason to feel elated. Idly he looked around the room, while he half listened to gun-fire in the distance, or the whine of rapidly-moving lorries on the street outside. Free Staters out for a raid on the home of some old comrade-in-arms. Lift your heart up, mother Erin! Well, for the time being, he was fairly nice and snug here, if it weren't for the never-ending commotion of the families who lived in the house. He glanced round to see how he was placed: the fireplace was big and clumsy, but when a fire blazed there, it was cosy and alluring. A fine settee, to hold two comfortably, stared at its dying embers now. A large mahogany table, on which he could spread out his work, undisturbed by scattered books, a yellow-varnished desk, with a few nests of file-cabinets, gave the room a look of a shy office not knowing what to do with itself. Beside the bed was an open two-shelved locker, one of thousands cast away by the Government when the war ended, and bought by Sean for half a crown; on the shelves were his soap, shaving-kit, face-flannel, and washbasin, all discreetly hidden by a coloured print curtain. On each side of the huge windows shelving held his many books, and the windows themselves were draped with long, creamy-coloured curtains of good twill. On the table stood the lamp that gave light to him when darkness came, and, in the centre, stood a mimosa plant, faded and dry now; never likely to show its delicate yellow blossoms again. He hadn't the gift of his mother in keeping flowers friendly and responsive. No picture hung on the wall yet, for he didn't care for the cheap ones on sale in the art shops, and he couldn't afford a good one yet. On the mantelshelf was a framed photograph of Thorwaldsen's *Venus*. On one side of the fireplace was a press in which he kept his crockery, coal, sticks for kindling, and a few saucepans. Beside this stood the small table holding his typewriter, and beside it, a suitable dignified chair to sit him straight up at his work. Not a lot to brag about, but enough for his present needs. A good nest, if it were not for the noise. The room to his right held a father, mother, and five children; the room over his head, the same with one more child: seven in the room beside him, eight in the one overhead

– his was a haven of peace, a place of dignity, compared with either of them.

SEAN O'CASEY, *Innisfallen Fare Thee Well*

DRAMA

The way I like garlic, the Irish like drama. It is no use telling me that too much garlic spoils some food; I dare say they are right, but I have never been able to get too much garlic, and mostly not enough. The Irish seem to feel that it is hard to get enough drama.

CLAUD COCKBURN, *I, Claud*

MORE LASTING

More lasting is Fame than the life of men,
    For tradition then may keep it young,
But more lasting still is the poet's pen,
    And the book that speaks with undying tongue.

DOUGLAS HYDE (Trans.), *Studies and Translations from the Irish*

A RICH LAND AND
A POOR PEOPLE

History is unfinished in this island; long since it has come to a stop in Surrey.

WILLIAM TREVOR, *Beyond the Pale*

APRIL 1827

13th . . . A gentle south-west wind. Sultry, cloud periods and bright patches. Soft clouds like fleeces on top of each other. From Cill Bhriocáin Mills I saw the Galtees west of Cathair. The eastern mountain looked flat, and the western peak was like the top of a volcano. A thin mist-like foam between me and them. The Déise mountains beckoning to me with their peaks up over Bearna na Gaoithe gap.

A rich land and a poor people. I ask you a question. Why is this?

The Diary of Humphrey O'Sullivan (Trans. Thomas de Bhaldraith)

LOOK NOT

Look not with pride at thy polished shoe,
Be not proud, too, of thy cloak so nice,
In humility walk the road afoot,
And always salute the poor man twice.

DOUGLAS HYDE (Trans.), *Studies and Translations from the Irish*

Irish dignity, Irish hospitality and the easy good manners which still charm the modern traveller have an historical explanation. Three times, at least, the native aristocracy was conquered and dispossessed; many fled from Ireland to exile in France or Spain, but many others remained, to be forced down by poverty and penal legislation to the economic level of the peasantry.

Until the famine, it was by no means uncommon for poor peasants in mud cabins to make wills bequeathing estates which had long ago been confiscated from their forefathers, and that figure of fun in Victorian days, the Irish beggar who claimed to be descended from kings, was very often speaking the truth.

CECIL WOODHAM-SMITH, *The Great Hunger*

23

from THREE MARCHING SONGS

Remember all those renowned generations,
They left their bodies to fatten the wolves,
They left their homesteads to fatten the foxes,
Fled to far countries, or sheltered themselves
In cavern, crevice, or hole,
Defending Ireland's soul.

Be still, be still, what can be said?
My father sang that song,
But time amends old wrong,
All that is finished, let it fade.

Remember all those renowned generations,
Remember all that have sunk in their blood,
Remember all that have died on the scaffold,
Remember all that have fled, that have stood,
Stood, took death like a tune
On an old tambourine.

Be still, be still, what can be said?
My father sang that song,
But time amends old wrong,
And all that's finished, let it fade.

Fail, and that history turns into rubbish,
All that great past to a trouble of fools;
Those that come after shall mock at O'Donnell,
Mock at the memory of both O'Neills,
Mock Emmet, mock Parnell,
All the renown that fell.

Be still, be still, what can be said?
My father sang that song,
But time amends old wrong,
And all that's finished, let it fade.

W. B. YEATS, *Collected Poems*

. . . for it is a fit house for an outlaw, a meet bed for a rebel, and an apt cloak for a thief. First the outlaw being for his many crimes and villainies banished from the towns and houses of honest men, and wandering in waste places far from danger of law, maketh his mantle his house, and under it covereth himself from the wrath of heaven, from the offence of the earth, and from the sight of men: when it raineth it is his pentice [i.e. cover], when it bloweth it is his tent, when it freezeth it is his tabernacle; in summer he can wear it loose, in winter he can wrap it close; at all times he can use it, never heavy, never cumbersome. Likewise for a rebel it is as serviceable: for in his war that he maketh (if at least it deserve the name of war) when he still flyeth from his foe and lurketh in the thick woods and straight passages waiting for advantages, it is his bed, yea and almost all his household stuff. For the wood is his house against all weathers, and his mantle is his cave to sleep in. There he wrappeth his self round and ensconceth himself strongly against the gnats, which in the country do more annoy the naked rebels whilst they keep the woods, and do more sharply wound them than all their enemies' swords or spears which can seldom come nigh them; yea and oftentimes their mantle serveth them when they are near driven, being wrapped about their left arm instead of a target, for it is hard to cut through it with a sword; besides, it is light to bear, light to throw away, and being as they then commonly are naked, it is to them all in all. Lastly, for a thief it is so handsome, as it may seem it was first invented for him, for under it he can cleanly convey any fit pillage that cometh handsomely in his way, and when he goeth abroad in the night on freebooting [i.e., plundering] it is his best and surest friend, for lying as they often do, two or three nights together abroad to watch for their booty, with that they can prettily shroud themselves under a bush or a bankside till they may conveniently do their errand. And when all is done he can, in his mantle, pass through any town or company, being close hooded over his head as he useth from knowledge of any to whom he is endangered. Besides all this he or any man else that is disposed to mischief or villainy may, under his mantle, go privily, armed without suspicion of any, carry his headpiece, his skene [i.e. dagger] or pistol, if he please to be always in a readiness. Thus necessary and fitting is a mantle for a bad man. And surely for a bad housewife it is no less convenient. For some of them that be these wandering women, called of them *Monashut*, it is half a wardrobe, for in summer ye shall find her arrayed commonly but in her smock and mantle to be more ready for her light services; and in her travel it is her cloak and safeguard, and also a coverlet for her lewd exercise, and when she hath filled her vessel, under it she can hide both her burden and her blame; yea, and when her bastard is born it serves instead of all her swaddling clothes, her mantles, her cradles with which others are vainly cumbered, and as for all other good women which love to do but little work, how handsome it is to lie in and sleep, or to louse themselves [i.e., *de*-louse themselves] in the sunshine, they that have been but a while in Ireland can well witness. Sure I am that ye will think it very unfit for good housewives to stir in or to busy herself about her housewifery in sort as they should. These be some of the abuses for which I would think it meet to forbid all mantles.

EDMUND SPENSER, *A View of the Present State of Ireland*

REGENCY DUKE

The following morning soon after ten o'clock he was summoned to breakfast with His Majesty. This was what the Duke had hoped for. A second servant announced that he must go immediately in his dressing-gown. The King plunged into amusing gossip. After a pause the Duke took courage and asked outright if His Majesty was as pleased with Irish conditions as was reported. Oh yes; but he thought that everything done for the Irish must be gradual. He could not interfere himself, for constitutional reasons. 'Here I got extremely interested and was going to say something on my mind, but that beast Sir Edmund Naylor [Sir George Nayler] came in.' Before the subject could be resumed the King sent his guest with Lord Francis Conyngham to look at the Pavilion in detail. It was magnificent, and the Duke found the steam contrivances in the kitchen perfection, particularly one for keeping food warm on an iron table. For dinner the King had the Music Room fully lighted for the Duke's sake. It was like an oriental fairy tale. The band were playing Rossini. Hart was made to waltz with Lady Cowper.

At breakfast the following morning the King began again to burble about trivialities. What horse did the Duke ride? What did he think of the steam engine? He spoke of his yacht, its size, the merit of steam-propelled boats and the difficulty of navigating those with rigging. On his return from the state visit to Ireland he had been totally without fresh water. The Duke did not like to interrupt. At last the King touched upon the cruelties and disturbances in Ireland which were equal to the worst atrocities of savages. To remedy such horrors was not a question of Catholic versus Protestant, but of gradual improvement of education and amelioration of conditions. Here the Duke fancied the opportunity to press his point had at last arrived. But he could not get the King to stop talking. He just managed to convey that there were several matters he wished to discuss with him privately. At this point Francis Conyngham tactfully withdrew. Rather nervously the guest begged the King to follow up his highly successful visit to Ireland by granting some elementary concessions to the Catholics. Whereupon the King said he was not in the habit of talking politics, confided that his father's madness had been caused by worry over the Irish question, and by a deliberate process of parrying avoided committing himself. The Duke nevertheless thanked the King for his confidence while reminding him that he had been educated in certain political principles which it would be dishonourable to abjure. The King replied with great warmth. He considered him, the Duke, the spokesman of the most respectable profession of Whig principles. 'Good God, Hart,' he said, taking his arm, 'Sir, you shall hear me,' as though the Duke had not been listening respectfully to a non-stop monologue, and started all over again. The conversation lasted for three and a half hours. On its conclusion they embraced.

JAMES LEES MILNE, The Bachelor Duke

AN IMPRISONING MYTH

The plague is a metaphor for conditions created by men and women, and men and women who have quarrelled can learn through suffering how to live together and apart, as France and Germany have learned. People can wake up in the morning and find an imprisoning myth no longer imprisoning but just plain silly. Cathleen ní Houlihan and King Billy are not necessarily immortal.

CONOR CRUISE O'BRIEN, *States of Ireland*

Dearest Old Darling – The one thing I have gained by my exile is the privilege of writing a letter, but theres very little to say, as I do not suppose that an 'essay on prison life' would pass the Censor, however interesting and amusing it might be. What you have called my 'misplaced sense of humour' still remains to me and I am quite well and cheerfull. I saw myself – for the first time for over three months the other day. It is quite amusing to meet yourself as a stranger. We bowed and grinned, and I thought my teeth very dirty, and very much wanting a dentist, and I'd got very thin and very sunburnt. In six months I shall not recognise myself at all my memory of faces is so bad. I remember a fairy tale of a Princess, who banished mirrors when she began to grow old. I think it showed a great want of interest in life. The less I see my face the more curious I grow about it, and I dont resent it growing old. Its queer and lonely here. There was so much life in Mountjoy. There were seaguls, and pigeons – which I had quite tame; there were 'Stop Press' cries, little boys splashing in the canal, and singing Irish songs shrill and discordant, but with such vigour. There was a black spaniel too with long silky ears, and a most attractive convict baby with a squint – and soft Irish voices everywhere. There were the trains 'Broadstone and Northwall' trams, and even an old melodion and a man trying to play an Irish tune on a bugle over the wall! Here its so still and I find it awfully difficult to understand what anyone says to me, and they seem to find the same trouble with me. 'English as she is spoke' can be very puzzling. One thing nice here is the Holy hocks in the garden, they seem to understand gardening. There is a great crop of carrots too that we pass every day, going to 'exercise' round and round in a ring – like so many old hunters in the summer.

I had such a lovely journey over here. My escort never had been on the sea before and kept thinking she was going to be ill. I lay down and enjoyed a sunny porthole and a fresh breeze. There was a big air ship – like the picture of a Zeppelin cruising about when we arrived. I was awfully pleased as I never saw one. I'd love to dive in a submarine. I dreamt of you the other night. You had on a soft looking small blue (dark) hat and it was crooked. You had bought tickets and three donkeys and were going to take Esther and I to Egypt of all places! When I woke up I had to laugh, but it was wonderfully vivid. Look it up in a 'dream book'. I dream a great deal ever since I was in jail and never hardly did before.

I'd love to show you all the dogrel I wrote in Mountjoy, though I know you'd only jeer in a kindly way. I love writing it so, and I've not lost it its in my head all right. Whens your next book coming out, and the one with some of my pictures if it ever does. They were very bad. I can do much better now . . . was just beginning to get some feeling into my black and white when I left Ireland. I made quils out of rooks tail feathers that I found in the garden, they are much nicer than most pens – you can get such a fine soft line.

Now darling again I repeat dont worry about me. I am quite cheerful and content, and would really have felt very small and useless if I had been ignored. I am quite patient and believe that everything will happen for the best. One thing I should enjoy getting out for, and that would be to see the faces of respectable people when I met them! I dont like to send anyone my love for fear that most valuable offering would be spurned. I expect though Molly has a soft spot for me somewhere. Very best love to Esther and to Susan and to all of the 'rebelly crew', if ever you come across them. Do go to the Transport Union headquarters if ever you go to Dublin, theyd all think you were me and love to see you and you could tell them about me. Now best love, old darling and send me a budget of news and gossip, when you can write, about all my pals, and my family, and any things amusing at all.

I laugh when I think of Mordaunt! and Mabel –

Yrs. Con———(vict G.12)

Letter from CONSTANCE DE MARKIEVICZ to her sister from prison

DOREEN! DOREEN!
*(For Lady Brabourne, killed with Lord
Mountbatten)*

I remember the summer when she went away,
our last magnolia had died that year
and the embothrium broke into a red flame.
The brambles were hanging across the roadway
when she waved goodbye with Mrs Congreve;
the land was singing, calling her back again.

Little did we know that time would find her
torn apart by the sorrow of our history.
O, they killed the Lord of Sligo's daughter
as she bathed her memories in the calm sea!
Her death's a grave that keeps filling with water
where we must bathe for love, incessantly.

THOMAS MCCARTHY, The Sorrow Garden

One harsh, dark March afternoon a squealing hinge made me look through the kitchen window. A young man was entering the cobbled yard from the abandoned cinema, which meant that he had climbed our eight-foot garden wall. Yet I felt not at all alarmed, possibly because I was never prone to be made uneasy by the unconventional. Or it may simply have been because the young man looked so amiable and vulnerable. As he stood at the back door I noticed that he seemed rather apprehensive and very tired. He was tall, broad-shouldered and handsome, and I marked a Kerry brogue when he gave his name as Pat Carney and asked, diffidently, if he might see one or both of my parents.

In the living-room my mother's bath chair was close to the sulky wartime fire of wet turf. She seemed oddly unsurprised by our visitor's original approach route and my curiosity was further sharpened when she asked me to leave her alone with Pat. Ten minutes later Pat was back in the kitchen. He said that he had been invited to stay for a few days and that my mother would like to speak to me. Then, pausing inside the living-room door, I did begin to feel alarmed. Never before had I seen my mother looking so distraught. Mrs Mansfield and San Toy were coming to tea so there was no time to waste on euphemisms. In a couple of sentences I had been told that Pat was on the run, wanted for the murder of a Dublin detective-sergeant. He had come to us as a protégé of my father's elder sister who, never having recognised the validity of the post-Treaty Irish government, was an active member of the illegal IRA. On no account must any caller be allowed to see our guest or any trace of his presence. As I continued to stand by the door, paralysed with astonishment, my mother made a gallant preliminary bid to sort out the ethics of the situation. 'This young man is a criminal though he regards himself as a patriot. No doubt his elders are chiefly to blame. They are using his muddled, foolish idealism. But we can talk about it later. Now please show him his room and give him a meal.'

I walked down the hall in a joyous daze. This was the stuff of which fantasies are made, yet now it had become part of the reality of my own life. I was to prepare a meal for a man on the run who would be hanged if caught. My mother might have saved her breath. Of course Pat was not a criminal, or muddled or foolish. He was a most glorious patriot, heroically dedicated to the reunification of Ireland. No one had ever suggested that my grandfather and father were criminals because they belonged to the Old IRA. One had to be logical. I was badly jolted when I discovered how strongly my father disapproved of Pat. But then I reflected that he (my father) was very old (forty-three). And I made allowances for the fact that at that age some people just can't have the right reactions any more.

Listening to my parents, I gathered that for some days they had been half-expecting Pat without knowing exactly why he was on the run. Now they were disagreeing vigorously about how they should deal with him and it gave me a certain sardonic satisfaction to observe them both being inconsistent; at twelve, one likes the feet of clay to appear occasionally. My father should have been the one to welcome – or at least tolerate – Pat, while my mother (given her ancestry) should have been the one to reject him. Instead, my father coldly argued that it would be sinful to shelter someone who had deliberately killed an innocent man in the course of a seditious campaign against a lawfully established government. And my mother warmly argued that it was unthinkable, sinful or no, to betray someone whose coming to our home was an act of faith in our humanity. She insisted that allowances must be made for Pat's sick idealism. To which my father, sprung from generations of rebels, replied austerely that it would prove impossible to govern the state if hectic emotionalism were to be accepted as an excuse for murder. My mother then suggested that he should go at once to the gardai barracks and report on Pat's whereabouts. But he didn't.

My parents seem never to have debated the ethics of capital punishment; presumably they accepted it, in theory, as the appropriate penalty for murder. Yet had it not been employed in Ireland during the Forties, as part of the government's anti-IRA campaign, they might well have refused to succour Pat. When such a decision can lead directly to a death sentence it requires more moral courage, or moral arrogance, than either of my parents possessed.

From their point of view an awkward situation was being compounded by the need to impress on me that giving refuge to Pat did not mean condoning his crime. In the end they gave up pretending to unravel this tangled skein for my benefit, which was sensible of them since I well knew that they were incapable of unravelling it for their own. I had in any case already come to my own conclusions and was only listening to their dutiful dissertations out of politeness. Yet I vaguely sympathised with their discomfiture; though they repudiated Pat as a violent man their consciences compelled them to allow for the fact that he saw himself as a soldier fighting a just war – a dilemma that in present-day Northern Ireland has again become familiar to many.

Pat stayed with us for a fortnight, but he and I never referred directly to his peculiar status and he made no attempt to influence me politically. We played round after round of rummy and he gave me lessons in map-reading and taught me how to whistle through my fingers so piercingly that I can be heard two miles away. To me this marvellous companion seemed a magic sort of person, an intelligent grown-up who had retained all the wondering enthusiasms of childhood. And my intuition was right. It was Pat's tragedy that he had never outgrown either the innocence or the ruthlessness of youth.

My parents also became very fond of Pat and deeply concerned about him. Night after night they argued patiently in futile attempts to make him see the error of his ways. Soon he seemed a member of the family – quite an achievement, in view of the strains imposed on all the adults concerned by his presence in the house. Had he been detected under our roof, my father would not have perjured himself by denying any knowledge of his identity and so would certainly have been imprisoned – as his sister was soon to be, on Pat's account.

Our guest was careful never to go too near a window and any knock at the door sent him rushing upstairs. Remembering how I relished all this melodrama, I wonder now if I fully understood that we were truly dicing with death. But my light-hearted approach may well have helped by easing the tension generated between the three adults. Pat knew that I took the game seriously enough to keep all the rules, and I was made deliriously proud by his entrusting to me the addressing and posting of his letters. One morning I went into his room to leave fresh linen on the bed and saw an automatic by the pillow. For years this was to rank as the most thrilling moment in my life. I tingled all over at the romance of that weapon – symbol of Adventure! – gleaming black and lethal on the white sheet. It never occurred to me that in certain circumstances it could be used to kill the local gardai, the fathers of my playmates. But then it was impossible to associate the gentle, considerate Pat with any form of violence or cruelty.

One evening Pat said good-bye instead of good-night and when we got up next morning he was gone. We heard nothing of him for several months, but his luck did not hold. He was eventually captured in my aunt's house, while asleep, and tried in Dublin before the Military Tribunal. Then he was hanged by the neck until he died, at eight o'clock in the morning on December 1, 1944. His real name was Charles Kerins.

In Waterford city, where I was by then at school, December 1, 1944, was a morning of violent wind and slashing rain. Just before eight o'clock I was queuing for my breakfast. I knew of Pat's attitude towards his sentence and at the moment of his hanging, when the gong in the hall was signalling us to enter the refectory, I experienced an almost hysterical elation. Then, curiously enough, I ate my usual hearty meal. It was against the nationalist tradition in my blood to mourn such deaths, for that would have been to imply that the sacrifice was not worth while.

Our mail was distributed during the mid-morning break and two worlds met when I stood amongst my classmates and – while they chattered of hockey and drank their milk – read a letter from a friend who had been hanged three hours earlier. With his letter Pat had enclosed a silver ring made on the prison ship in Belfast by a comrade of his, 'Rocky' Burns, who was later shot dead in Belfast by the RUC – or perhaps the B specials. I wore the ring constantly from that moment until my fingers and my ideals outgrew it – developments which conveniently occurred at about the same time. But I have it still and I would not part with it.

DERVLA MURPHY, Wheels Within Wheels

Jack gave her a push that sent her sprawling onto the floor. He jumped out of the chair and was away out of the room.

'Roger.'

She heard his voice in the hall.

'Roger.'

She heard him almost wail outside in the road.

Roger's car drove off and then after a moment Jack followed. For some inexplicable reason he had his hand on the horn and she heard the blaring twist away along the road.

She got up from the floor.

How absurd we are, she thought. How easily we become affected by panic. I will be calm, domestic. I will clear away the signs of our panic. I will open the wine, bang the cushions, set straight the rugs, polish the glasses. They will be back soon and there will be no more panic.

Then there was the first explosion. The house shivered and the glass in the window cracked from the top down to the bottom, and shards, slivers, splinters, slid scattered across the floor.

JENNIFER JOHNSTONE, The Railway Station Man

JUST SO MUCH HISTORY

The Battle of Glenmama, the Convention of Drumceat. The Act of Settlement, the Renunciation Act. The Act of Union, the Toleration Act. Just so much history it sounds like now, yet people starved or died while other people watched. A language was lost, a faith forbidden. Famine followed revolt, plantation followed that. But it was people who were struck into the soil of other people's land, not forests of new trees; and it was greed and treachery that spread as a disease among them all. No wonder unease clings to these shreds of history and shots ring out in answer to the mockery of drums. No wonder the air is nervy with suspicion.

WILLIAM TREVOR, *Beyond the Pale*

GOD'S FAIR INNOCENTS

We never knew who might not come to the farm, but the three we hoped for, perhaps prayed for, never came.

The first was a harper, one who would play on a little old Irish harp like the harp of Brian Boru, that king from whom all the O'Briens are descended.

The second was Charles Stewart Parnell who was our hero. Bessie imagined him striding up to the front door, his beard waving in the wind, if it was long enough to wave, his eyes flashing.

'What would they be flashing about?' Janie asked in her quiet, practical voice.

'Me,' Bessie exclaimed, '*me!*' Then aside to Janie and very fast, 'he would have heard that on Lough Gur lives a young girl who would die for him! Wouldn't he want to see that young girl, silly?' Then she went on in what we called her oratorical voice, 'He is a man! a man worth dying for!'

'Who is worth dying for?' mother asked from the kitchen while Dooley left her dusting to listen.

'Mr Parnell,' we cried together.

'Och! *him!*' Dooley said with contempt. 'Descended from Sassenachs! Himself a Protestant and his mother from America! *Him!*'

'Oh!' Bessie shrieked, 'it isn't true, is it, mother? He is a pure Catholic Irishman? Say he is!' Bessie was hurling herself about the little room in excitement when a hand came through the open window and caught her by the arm; the voice of Father Burke of Limerick boomed round the room.

'*Hibernicis ipsis Hibernior*, that's what the man is, God bless him – for all his foreign blood which is none of his fault, and his heresy which please God we'll cure him of.'

MARY CARBERRY, *The Farm by Lough Gur*

. . . a small boy on another estate at the other side of County Wicklow was to have his imagination seared for ever by his gatekeeper's description of a poor countryman, at the end of a cart, being flogged on the belly instead of the back until his bowels hung down before him. In later years that lad, a traitor to his class, would tear to pieces the very structure of Whig Ascendancy.

His house is still there at the head of the beautiful Avoca valley on the road from Rathdrum to Arklow, a plain, solid Regency house now the property of the Forestry Commission. Charles Stewart Parnell himself is, like Swift, one of our very few rockets; a man so incomparably great that he throws a brilliant light on the very ordinary folk about him and invests with all the glamour of romance old feuds on which the eye of history would scarcely otherwise have lit. Yet even he, cold master of circumstance that he was, asked too much of the ragged battalions which he led.

No biographer has pierced the secret of his greatness; perhaps none ever will. They write of his coldness, but that is only a symptom. I have frequently thought that, as with Swift, it was the fear of insanity, and that it was this which gave him his unnatural detachment from ordinary human emotion, his mastery over men and lack of it over himself. What others envied he must have feared, and gone searching through the world for someone who could relieve him of his solitude.

FRANK O'CONNOR, *Munster, Leinster and Connaught*

Dante bent across the table and cried to Mr Casey:

– Right! Right! They were always right! God and morality and religion come first.

Mrs Dedalus, seeing her excitement, said to her:

– Mrs Riordan, don't excite yourself answering them.

– God and religion before everything! Dante cried. God and religion before the world!

Mr Casey raised his clenched fist and brought it down on the table with a crash.

– Very well, then, he shouted hoarsely, if it comes to that, no God for Ireland!

– John! John! cried Mr Dedalus, seizing his guest by the coat sleeve.

Dante stared across the table, her cheeks shaking. Mr Casey struggled up from his chair and bent across the table towards her, scraping the air from before his eyes with one hand as though he were tearing aside a cobweb.

– No God for Ireland! he cried. We have had too much God in Ireland. Away with God!

– Blasphemer! Devil! screamed Dante, starting to her feet and almost spitting in his face.

Uncle Charles and Mr Dedalus pulled Mr Casey back into his chair again, talking to him from both sides reasonably. He stared before him out of his dark flaming eyes, repeating:

– Away with God, I say!

Dante shoved her chair violently aside and left the table, upsetting her napkin ring which rolled slowly along the carpet and came to rest against the foot of an easy chair. Mrs Dedalus rose quickly and followed her towards the door. At the door Dante turned round violently and shouted down the room, her cheeks flushed and quivering with rage:

– Devil out of hell! We won! We crushed him to death! Fiend!

The door slammed behind her.

Mr Casey, freeing his arms from his holders, suddenly bowed his head on his hands with a sob of pain.

– Poor Parnell! he cried loudly. My dead king!

He sobbed loudly and bitterly.

Stephen raising his terror-stricken face, saw that his father's eyes were full of tears.

JAMES JOYCE, *Portrait of the Artist*

The situation in the north-east remains the old one – segregation, the inability of natives and settlers to live together as one society, the settlers' fear and their determination to hold exclusive power. This is now the cause of violence as it was in 1798.

It is as though the whole of Anglo-Irish history has been boiled down and its dregs thrown out, leaving their poisonous concentrate on these six counties.

DAVID THOMSON, *Woodbrook*

I am convinced that the distinct communities indicated by the terms 'Catholic' and 'Protestant' are the prime realities of the situation. This is not the same as saying that religion is the main factor. Religious affiliation, in Ireland, is the rule of thumb by which one can distinguish between the people of native, Gaelic stock (Catholic) and those of settler stock from Scotland and England (Protestant).

The area now known as Northern Ireland is the only part of Ireland where sizable populations of both stocks have long existed, and now exist, together. And in Northern Ireland they have functioned, and function, not just as religious groupings but as political groupings too. Protestant almost always means Unionist: favouring union that is, not with the rest of Ireland, but with Britain. Catholic almost always means anti-unionist, and implies support for some kind of united Ireland; this is not always conceived as incorporation in the present Republic, but the distinction is negligible, from a Protestant point of view.

In Northern Ireland, especially in conditions of tension, but also in normal times, the basic social information which people look for, in relation to any unfamiliar person or group, is 'religion'. The same person who may tell you that 'religion' is not important, or that its importance is exaggerated, will talk freely, or not freely, with a friend in a taxi, depending on whether or not he knows that the religion of the taxi driver is the same as that of the group to which he himself adheres.

In troubled times he may not take a taxi at all, unless he knows the driver personally, and can assess his reliability for a given drive, under given conditions of socio-religious stress. A well-known Catholic politician might take a Protestant taxi, even in conditions of tension, if he knew the driver and thought him safe. But if that driver took an unexpected turn into a Protestant street, the passenger would at least become tense, and not just about the fare. And both the driver and the passenger would be conscious, throughout the journey, of whether they were travelling along a Catholic or a Protestant street. And in no circumstances would either of them in the presence of the other allude to this situation, or to any subject bordering on politics or religion.

CONOR CRUISE O'BRIEN, States of Ireland

from FUNERAL RITES

I

I shouldered a kind of manhood
stepping in to lift the coffins
of dead relations.
They had been laid out

in tainted rooms,
their eyelids glistening,
their dough-white hands
shackled in rosary beads.

Their puffed knuckles
had unwrinkled, the nails
were darkened, the wrists
obediently sloped.

The dulse-brown shroud,
the quilted satin cribs:
I knelt courteously
admiring it all

as wax melted down
and veined the candles,
the flames hovering
to the women hovering

behind me.
And always, in a corner,
the coffin lid,
its nail-heads dressed

with little gleaming crosses.
Dear soapstone masks,
kissing their igloo brows
had to suffice

before the nails were sunk
and the black glacier
of each funeral
pushed away.

                    II
Now as news comes in
of each neighbourly murder
we pine for ceremony,
customary rhythms:

the temperate footsteps
of a cortège, winding past
each blinded home.
I would restore

the great chambers of Boyne,
prepare a sepulchre
under the cupmarked stones.
Out of side-streets and bye-roads

purring family cars
nose into line,
the whole country tunes
to the muffled drumming

of ten thousand engines.
Somnambulant women,
left behind, move
through emptied kitchens

imagining our slow triumph
towards the mounds.
Quiet as a serpent
in its grassy boulevard

the procession drags its tail
out of the Gap of the North
as its head already enters
the megalithic doorway.

SEAMUS HEANEY, Selected Poems

POOR IRELAND

Some queries proposed to the consideration of the public:

Whether there be upon earth any Christian or civilised people so beggardly wretched and destitute, as the common Irish?

Whether, nevertheless, there is any other people whose wants may be more easily supplied from home?

Whether, if there was a wall of brass a thousand cubits high round their kingdom, our natives might not nevertheless live cleanly and comfortably, till the land, and reap the fruits of it?

Whether an Irish lady, set out with French silks and Flanders lace, may not be said to consume more beef and butter than fifty of our labouring peasants?

Whether there be any country in Christiandom more capable of improvement than Ireland?

Whether the maxim, 'What is everybody's business is nobody's business', prevails in any country under the sun more than in Ireland?

Whether we are the only people who starve in the market of plenty?

Whether there be not every year more cash circulated at the card-tables of Dublin than at all the fairs of Ireland?

Whose fault is it if poor Ireland continues poor?

GEORGE BERKELEY, Bishop of Cloyne, *The Querist*

THE GREAT HUNGER

The famine left hatred behind. Between Ireland and England the memory of what was done and endured has lain like a sword. Other famines followed, as other famines had gone before, but it is the terrible years of the Great Hunger which are remembered, and only just beginning to be forgiven.

CECIL WOODHAM-SMITH, *The Great Hunger*

The old Irish race never built a town – so we are told by Arland Ussher, the Gaelic scholar, though the assertion is naturally disputed – and one of the more ingenious grudges held in Ireland against the British is that they never taught the Irish how to do so. Much of what the Irish had – the castles, mills, warehouses, forts, churches, farms – was ruined by wars and by abandonment, so that when we turn from climate to history, we are passing through a land where, in the name of some violent dream or other, real things have been destroyed.

V. S. PRITCHETT, *At Home and Abroad*

FAILED FRENCH INVASION (1796)

All over Europe, people felt the harsh breath of the east wind. In Paris and London people were found frozen to death in the streets. In Ireland, the Irish army, bracing themselves for the invasion, were caught in a blizzard. At Bandon the militia, led by their colonel, twenty-seven-year-old Lord Castlereagh, huddled for shelter in a deserted church; at Birr the peasantry were set to dig the artillery out of the snowdrifts; and in Dublin, the garrison was issued with flannel waistcoats specially sewn by ladies of the viceregal court.

But the hurricane blew, scattering the French fleet, and one

of the great Cork magnates, Lord Shannon, hummed the lines
from 'Lillibulero'. It was a Protestant wind.

THOMAS PAKENHAM, *Year of Liberty*

THE SPUDS WILL BLOOM

BRIDGET: They say that's the way it snakes in, don't they? First
the smell; and then one morning the stalks are all black
and limp.

DOALTY: Are you stupid? It's the rotting stalks makes the sweet
smell for God's sake. That's what the smell is – rotting
stalks.

MAIRE: Sweet smell! Sweet smell! Every year at this time
somebody comes back with stories of the sweet smell.
Sweet God, did the potatoes ever fail in Baile Beag? Well,
did they ever – ever? Never! There was never blight here.
Never. Never. But we're always sniffing about for it, aren't
we? – looking for disaster. The rents are going to go up
again – the harvest's going to be lost – the herring have
gone away for ever – there's going to be evictions. Honest
to God, some of you people aren't happy unless you're
miserable and you'll not be right content until you're
dead!

DOALTY: Bloody right, Maire. And sure St Colmcille prophesied
there'd never be blight here. He said:
     The spuds will bloom in Baile Beag
     Till rabbits grow an extra lug.
And sure that'll never be. So we're all right.

BRIAN FRIEL, *Translations*

POVERTY

The back door of our house was not locked until the farm-boys
had gone out after prayers. Once or twice a tall, unkempt
woman came in with a baby bundled under her arm. Her black

hair hung over her neck and shoulders and partly hid her oval face which would have been handsome but for the hard bitterness of her mouth. No one knew who the tragic creature was, although it was rumoured that she had been sent back from America as a bad character. She came always in dusk or darkness, usually when we were at prayers, giving no greeting, speaking no word as she walked to the fire and poured boiling water into her teapot from kettle or saucepan, never putting down the baby but shifting it from one arm to the other as she went about her preparations. One of the maids would get up from her knees to put a jug of milk within her reach, otherwise she seemed to have all she needed in her basket. The baby made neither movement nor sound, nor did the woman unwrap it to give it food, in fact one wondered if the bundle under her arm was a baby at all. She went as she came, silent and unexplained, into the night.

MARY CARBERRY, *The Farm by Lough Gur*

BEGGING IN DUBLIN

Till afternoon I held my face raised towards the southern sky, then towards the western till night. The bowl gave me a lot of trouble. I couldn't use my hat because of my skull. As for holding out my hand, that was quite out of the question. So I got a tin and hung it from a button of my greatcoat, what's the matter with me, of my coat, at pubis level. It did not hang plumb, it leaned respectfully towards the passer-by, he had only to drop his mite. But that obliged him to come up close to me, he was in danger of touching me. In the end I got a bigger tin, a kind of big tin box, and I placed it on the sidewalk at my feet. But people who give alms don't much care to toss them, there's something contemptuous about this gesture which is repugnant to sensitive natures. To say nothing of their having to aim. They are prepared to give, but not for their gift to go rolling under the passing feet or under the passing wheels, to be picked up perhaps by some undeserving person. So they don't give. There are those, to be sure, who stoop, but generally speaking people who give alms don't much care to stoop. What they like above all is to sight the wretch from afar, get ready their penny, drop it in their stride and hear the God bless you dying away in the distance. Personally I never said that, nor anything like it, I wasn't much of a believer, but I did make a noise with my mouth. In the end I got a kind of board or tray and tied it to my neck and waist. It jutted out just at the right height, pocket height, and its edge was far enough from my person for the coin to be bestowed without danger. Some days I strewed it with flowers, petals, buds and that herb which men call fleabane, I believe, in a word whatever I could find. I didn't go out of my way to look for them, but all the pretty things of this description that came my way were for the board. They must have thought I loved nature.

SAMUEL BECKETT, *The Expelled*

The 'Prosecutor for the Crown' told us: a multitude of criminal cases in the south of Ireland have their origin in the desire to possess land. In that part of Ireland there is no manufacturing, no industry, the people have only the land to live off, and, as they are accustomed at all times to live on the least that a man can subsist on, when a man has no land he really faces death. That is why implacable hatred and numberless acts of violence are born of *evictions*.

ALEXIS DE LA TOCQUEVILLE, *Journey in Ireland*

THE BLACKBIRD
(*after the Irish, twelfth century*)

A blackbird breaks the silence
With frantic cries of grief.
His nest is torn and trampled,
The bones of his young are scattered.

Frail bird, I'll tell you this:
I know something of what you feel.
When it comes to hurt in homes
There's little for you to teach.

A lout climbed up and smashed
Your home and heart in a flash.
The careful curves of your nest
Are mere twigs to a man like that.

Your little ones came when you called,
Clustered on a steady branch.
Not one of them needs you now:
Nettles thrive where you sang.

Your mate was beside you always,
Her beak a bright nib of light
When that man sprung his trap
And she died, her wings sapped.

I find it hard, dear God, to bear
With all that you make happen.
It sometimes seems that others thrive
While all I build lies in tatters.

Grief holds me like a shawl
Weighing me down as I walk.
Nothing I say can change things.
Nothing can mend that wounded branch.

SEAN DUNNE, *The Sheltered Nest*

EVICTIONS

Two recent attempts to carry out evictions on the island came
to nothing, for each time a sudden storm rose, by, it is said,
the power of a native witch, when the steamer was approaching, and made it impossible to land.

This morning, however, broke beneath a clear sky of June,
and when I came into the open air the sea and rocks were
shining with wonderful brilliancy. Groups of men, dressed in
their holiday clothes, were standing about, talking with anger
and fear, yet showing a lurking satisfaction at the thought of
the dramatic pageant that was to break the silence of the seas.

About half-past nine the steamer came in sight, on the narrow line of sea-horizon that is seen in the centre of the bay, and immediately a last effort was made to hide the cows and sheep of the families that were most in debt.

Till this year no one on the island would consent to act as bailiff, so that it was impossible to identify the cattle of the defaulters. Now, however, a man of the name of Patrick has sold his honour, and the effort of concealment is practically futile.

This falling away from the ancient loyalty of the island has caused intense indignation, and early yesterday morning, while I was dreaming on the Dun, this letter was nailed on the doorpost of the chapel:

'Patrick, the devil, a revolver is waiting for you. If you are missed with the first shot, there will be five more that will hit you.

'Any man that will talk with you, or work with you, or drink a pint of porter in your shop, will be done with the same way as yourself.'

As the steamer drew near I moved down with the men to watch the arrival, though no one went further than about a mile from the shore.

Two curaghs from Kilronan with a man who was to give help in identifying the cottages, the doctor, and the relieving officer, were drifting with the tide, unwilling to come to land without the support of the larger party. When the anchor had been thrown it gave me a strange throb of pain to see the boats being lowered, and the sunshine gleaming on the rifles and helmets of the constabulary who crowded into them.

Once on shore the men were formed in close marching order, a word was given, and the heavy rhythm of their boots came up over the rocks. We were collected in two straggling bands on either side of the roadway, and a few moments later the body of magnificent armed men passed close to us, followed by a low rabble, who had been brought to act as drivers for the sheriff.

After my weeks spent among primitive men this glimpse of the newer types of humanity was not reassuring. Yet these mechanical police, with the commonplace agents and sheriffs, and the rabble they had hired, represented aptly enough the civilisation for which the homes of the island were to be desecrated.

A stop was made at one of the first cottages in the village, and the day's work began. Here, however, and at the next cottage, a compromise was made, as some relatives came up at the last moment and lent the money that was needed to gain a respite.

In another case a girl was ill in the house, so the doctor interposed, and the people were allowed to remain after a merely formal eviction. About midday, however, a house was reached where there was no pretext for mercy, and no money could be procured. At a sign from the sheriff the work of carrying out the beds and utensils was begun in the middle of a crowd of natives who looked on in absolute silence, broken only by the wild imprecations of the woman of the house. She belonged to one of the most primitive families on the island, and she shook with uncontrollable fury as she saw the strange armed men who spoke a language she could not understand driving her from the hearth she had brooded on for thirty years. For these people the outrage to the hearth is the supreme catastrophe. They live here in a world of grey, where there are wild rains and mists every week in the year, and their warm chimney corners, filled with children and young girls, grow into the consciousness of each family in a way it is not easy to understand in more civilised places.

The outrage to a tomb in China probably gives no greater shock to the Chinese than the outrage to a hearth in Inishmaan gives to the people.

When the few trifles had been carried out, and the door blocked with stones, the old woman sat down by the threshold and covered her head with her shawl.

Five or six other women who lived close by sat down in a circle round her, with mute sympathy. Then the crowd moved on with the police to another cottage where the same scene was to take place, and left the group of desolate women sitting by the hovel.

There were still no clouds in the sky, and the heat was intense. The police when not in motion lay sweating and gasping under the walls with their tunics unbuttoned. They were not attractive, and I kept comparing them with the islandmen, who walked up and down as cool and fresh-looking as the sea-gulls.

J. M. SYNGE, *The Aran Islands*

Ireland, it has been said, is a land of endless enchantments or as narrow as a pig's back. It all depends on the way you happen to be feeling about it at the moment. The enchantments, apart from sudden orgies of wild beauty among mountains and lakes and lake-islands, are often intangible as a dream: the narrowness of the pig's back can have, at countless moments of despair, the claustrophobic reality of a nightmare, and this may be why many of the people, generally of a natural cheerfulness of disposition, are so often inclined to run away from their country or to die for her. Both these ingrown habits are, of course, methods of escape from an obsession; no country in the world, having produced so little on her own soil, is more absorbed by her own image; no people in the world more bemused by their own reflection in the glass; no nation less interested in the doings or the destinies of other nations; and for these shortcomings, if they are admitted to exist at all, there will always be a host of voluble excuses.

Ah for God's sake, look at our history!

MICHAEL MAC LIAMMOIR, *Ireland*

THE BEAUTY OF THE WORLD

The beauty of the world hath made me sad,
This beauty that will pass;
Sometimes my heart hath shaken with great joy
To see a leaping squirrel in a tree,
Or a red ladybird upon a stalk,
Or little rabbits in a field at evening,
Lit by a slanting sun,
Or some green hill where shadows drifted by,
Some quiet hill where mountainy man hath sown
And soon would reap; near to the gate of Heaven;
Or children with bare feet upon the sands

49

Of some ebbed sea, or playing on the streets
Of little towns in Connacht,
Things young and happy.
And then my heart hath told me:
These will pass,
Will pass and change, will die and be no more,
Things bright and green, things young and happy;
And I have gone upon my way
Sorrowful.

PATRICK PEARSE, written on the eve of his execution, 1916

A LYRICAL LANDSCAPE

WINDHARP
for Patrick Collins

The sounds of Ireland,
that restless whispering
you never get away
from, seeping out of
low bushes and grass,
heatherbells and fern,
wrinkling bog pools,
scraping tree branches,
light hunting cloud,
sound hounding sight,
a hand ceaselessly
combing and stroking
the landscape, till
the valley gleams
like the pile upon
a mountain pony's coat.

JOHN MONTAGUE, *New Selected Poems*

WINTER

Scél lem dúib:
   dordaid dam,
snigid gaim,
   ro fáith sam.

I have news for you: the stag bellows, winter snows, summer has gone.

Gáeth ard úar,
   ísel grían;
gair a rrith,
   ruirthech rían.

The wind is high and cold, the sun is low; its course is brief, the tide runs high.

Rorúad raith,
   ro cleth cruth,
ro gab gnáth
   giugrann guth.

The bracken has reddened, its shape has been hidden; the wild goose has raised his customary cry.

ro gab úacht	*Cold has caught the wings of birds; it is the*
etti én;	*time of ice – these are my news.*
aigrid ré –	
é mo scél.	

FRANK O'CONNOR (Trans.), *Irish Poetry AD 600–1200*

DOG'S TOOTH BAY

Walk down from the village to Dog's Bay in August – the time when Roundstone is most frequently visited – and you will be astonished at the profusion of blossom which occupies the little boggy fields set among bosses of glaciated pinkish granite – masses of white Ox-eye Daisies, of yellow Water Ragwort, and sheets of Purple Loosestrife and Marsh Woundwort; while on drier or more exposed ground rounded bushes of the smaller Furze, *Ulex Gallii*, covered with golden blossom, are almost overwhelmed by the purple profusion of Heather and of St Dabeoc's Heath. Down by the sea, where the limy sand, scattered far by winter gales, has turned the heath vegetation into short green grass, the sward is gay with Harebells and Squinancywort, and the air fragrant with the delicious scent of the Autumnal Lady's-tresses.

Here, at the landward end of the curve of Gorteen Bay, you come unexpectedly on a little lonely graveyard, with the sand in front and far-stretching undulating velvety grass behind, nibbled close by sheep and rabbits. The beauty of the spot has always affected me strangely, and I venture to repeat what I have written of it elsewhere: When I first knew this place, the cemetery was unenclosed and open to every wandering creature; now a decent though unattractive wall surrounds it. The only benefit the wall has conferred is to allow the wild-flowers to grow tall and to bloom unchecked. A peaceful spot; and since one has to die, what an enviable place for a long sleep, with the clear Atlantic waves breaking close at hand on the white sand, the Sea-Holly and Great Knapweed spreading more and more among the crosses, and the plovers and gulls passing to and fro across the sky. If one might be permitted to rest on so delectable a couch, it might seem almost worth the bother of dying.

PRAEGER, *The Way that I Went*

MOSSBAWN

To this day, green, wet corners, flooded wastes, soft rushy bottoms, any place with the invitation of watery ground and tundra vegetation, even glimpsed from a car or a train, possess an immediate and deeply peaceful attraction. It is as if I am betrothed to them, and I believe my betrothal happened one summer evening, thirty years ago, when another boy and myself stripped to the white country skin and bathed in a moss-hole, treading the liver-thick mud, unsettling a smoky muck off the bottom and coming out smeared and weedy and darkened. We dressed again and went home in our wet clothes, smelling of the ground and the standing pool, somehow initiated.

SEAMUS HEANEY, *Preoccupations*

AN EIGHTEENTH-CENTURY VIEW

I have a closet to my bedchamber, the window of which looks upon a fine lake *inhabited by swans*, beyond it and on each side are pretty hills, some covered with wood and others with cattle. On the side of one of the hills is a gentleman's house with a pigeon-house belonging to it, that embellishes the prospect very much.

About half a mile off is a pretty wood which formerly was enriched with very fine oaks and several other forest trees (it covers a hill of about twenty acres); it is now only a thicket of the young shoots from *their venerable stocks*, but it is very thick, and has the finest carpeting of violets, primroses, and meadow sweet, with innumerable inferior shrubs and weeds, which make such a *mass of colouring* as is delightful. But thorny and dangerous are the paths, for with these sweets are interwoven *treacherous nettles* and *outrageous brambles*! but the Dean has undertaken to clear away those usurpers and has already made some progress: it is called Wood Island, though it is no more than a peninsula; the large lake that almost surrounds it is often covered with threescore couple of swans at a time.

On the other side of the lake are hills of various shapes, and on the side of one of them the town of Down. The ruins of the old cathedral are on an eminence just opposite to Wood Island, from whence I have taken a drawing D.D. is making a path round the wood large enough to drive a coach; in some places it is so thick as to make it gloomy in the brightest day; in other places a view of the lake opens, and most of the trees are embroidered with woodbine and the *'flaunting eglantine'*. Four extraordinary seats are already made, one in an oak the other three in ash-trees. This afternoon we proposed spending some hours there, but the rain drove us back again; on the beach of the lake are a great many pretty cockle shells, which will not be neglected when the weather will permit me to go to it.

Mrs Delaney's Letters (2 June 1745)

THE DEAD

A few light taps upon the pane made him turn to the window. It had begun to snow again. He watched sleepily the flakes, silver and dark, falling obliquely against the lamplight. The time had come for him to set out on his journey westward. Yes, the newspapers were right: snow was general all over Ireland. It was falling on every part of the dark central plain, on the treeless hills, falling softly upon the Bog of Allen and, farther westward, softly falling into the dark mutinous Shannon waves. It was falling, too, upon every part of the lonely churchyard on the hill where Michael Furey lay buried. It lay thickly drifted on the crooked crosses and headstones, on the spears of the little gate, on the barren thorns. His soul swooned slowly as he heard the snow falling faintly through the universe and faintly falling, like the descent of their last end, upon all the living and the dead.

JAMES JOYCE, *Dubliners*

A STRETCH OF LIMESTONE COUNTRY

Up in the north-east corner of County Cork is a stretch of limestone country – open, airy, not quite flat; it is just perceptibly tilted from north to south, and the fields undulate in a smooth flowing way. Dark knolls and screens of trees, the network of hedges, abrupt stony ridges, slate glints from roofs give the landscape a featured look – but the prevailing impression is, emptiness. This is a part of Ireland with no lakes, but the sky's movement of clouds reflects itself everywhere as it might on water, rounding the trees with bloom and giving the grass a sheen. In the airy silence, any sound travels a long way. The streams and rivers, sunk in their valleys, are not seen until you come down to them.

ELIZABETH BOWEN, *Bowen's Court*

CANVAS BOATS

I must sing the praises of the *curach* or curragh, the canvas boat used everywhere along the western coast of Ireland for inshore fishing, lobster work, and as the usual means of communication in the island regions. Originally the covering was of hide; nowadays tarred canvas has replaced this. The framework is sometimes still made of rough hazel saplings, spaced a few inches apart; but light sawn slats like slating-laths are now often seen. The solid gunwale has thole-pins, on which the oars, with blades only three inches wide, are fixed. The bow rises high, like a pointed spoon; the stern is broad and square; and there is no keel at all, the boat being semicircular in section. Each man – and there are one-man, two-man and three-man curraghs – wields two oars. If a novice attempts to row one of these boats, it merely spins round, even in the absence of wind, until he gets the hang of it: and he barks his knuckles in addition, since the oars overlap, and must be kept one above the other. But the extreme lightness of these curraghs and the raised bow make them extraordinarily seaworthy in the hands of the men of the west, who will put to sea in them when the crew of many a larger boat might hesitate. They dance over the waves like corks, with a motion which is surprisingly rapid.

PRAEGAR, *The Way that I Went*

ANTONY

I looked after the ancient otter-hunter with envy. How lowly would he be estimated in the eyes of a Cheapside fisherman; one who wears a modest-coloured jacket, lest a showy garment might annoy the plethoric animals he is dabbling for – whose white basket is constructed of the finest wicker-work – with rods and reels, floats and flies, pastes and patties, lines and liqueurs sufficient to load a donkey – how contemptuously would he look down upon honest Antony! Figure to yourself a little feeble man, dressed in a jerkin of coarse blue cloth, with an otter (a fancy of my cousin's) blazoned on his arm: in one hand he holds a fish-spear, which assists him when he meets with rugged ground, in the other, a very unpretending angle, jointed rudely with a pen-knife, and secured by waxen threads; a *cast* of flies are wound about his hat, and his remaining stock, not exceeding half-a-dozen, are contained between the leaves of a tattered song-book: in the same depository he has some silk, dyed mohair, a hare's ear, and a few feathers from the cock, brown turkey, and mallard; and these simple materials furnish him with most efficient flies, but he requires a bright day to fabricate them, as his sight is indifferent.

W. H. MAXWELL, *Wild Sports of the West*

Looking round me in this year (1888) I found I had a little field of rough land in the upper part of my holding, and I determined to break it up, for it was very old land and useless as it was, and in my enthusiasm I purposed to break in half of it that year and the other half the year after.

Often a man has made an unprofitable plan, though at other times it doesn't turn out like that. This plan of mine wasn't worth much, for it resulted in a great deal of labour for me, and I gained little from all my work. I must set my face to the strand to get weed for manure; I had an old black ass, and he had to travel a mile and a half under every load, every step of it uphill.

Well, often has a man taken on a job, and before he'd had it long in hand he's found that he's had enough of it, and certainly that was the way with me. Very soon I was sick of it, more particularly as the old black ass was letting me down.

In the end I set half of the little field with potatoes. When I was planting them my father was in good trim; he was seventy years of age, and all that was wrong with him was that he was a bit bent. However, he used to pay a visit to this field every day, though he was getting weaker and slower every day.

Before long he began to give up his visits to the field altogether, though he was keen enough about it at first. One day, when I imagined he was in the field, I looked out and I couldn't see a sign of him there, and that struck me as odd. I asked a lad who was going by for news of him, and he said that he was in the house of Kate, his daughter, and sure enough there I found him.

'Father,' I said to him, 'wasn't I thinking that it was in the little field you were since you had your morning meal?'

'I don't hanker after it much,' said he.

'But you had a great fancy for it at first.'

'I had, but I don't feel like that now. I shan't see a potato come up in that field.'

There are many things we don't heed until it's too late. And after my father was buried I regretted that I hadn't questioned him and asked him whether he had seen or heard anything in the field when he visited it. No doubt, something of the kind happened to him, considering that he dated his life's end so accurately.

My father was in the grave before the potatoes showed above the ground. That left more of the world's trouble on poor Tomás; and that wasn't the end of my troubles either.

Round about Mayday there were mackerel to be caught that year, and we made a good penny out of them. I had five pounds put by at the end of a single week. Then my father died, and I had to take my five pounds and coffin him with them. Coffins weren't as dear in those days as they are to-day. The whole funeral cost about ten pounds then. It has often cost thirty pounds since then.

After I had gone through all this I had to wring more work out of my bones, and after all my toil working the little field there weren't two sackfuls of potatoes in it; only I got three crops of oats from it and the last crop was the best of them.

I set about the other side of the little field the next year, and I made a great deal more profit out of this half than out of the other that I had broken up first, for I had more experience of the nature of the soil, and I arranged my manuring to suit it.

TOMAS O'CROHAN, *The Island Man* (Trans. Robin Flower)

THE INOCULATOR

In the mountains I fell in with a man who had the air of being something of a *bon vivant*. He told me that his profession was that of inoculator, and that he was about to inoculate the children of the peasantry in this wild country. He assured me positively that of 361 children inoculated by him this year only one died. When it is understood that if he has been unfortunate enough to have a child die on his hands, not only is he not paid, but he must escape promptly in order to avoid a beating by the afflicted parents, it will be seen that the poor devil must take great pains with his patients. I have often thought that this practice of the peasantry would not be a bad one to introduce into towns, to encourage the doctors, to whom the death or cure of their patients is indifferent, for they are sure to be paid in either case, and are never beaten.

In travelling beside this decent creature, who appeared to be very light-hearted, he told me his whole story. He was born in this country, and had been brought up by his poor parents with the intention that he should enter the Church, the while depending for aid and protection on a rich man, who unfortunately died at Dublin. Finding himself then without friends, without promise of aid and without money, he thought for some time how he could employ himself. It was just the time when inoculation had begun to be put into practice, and the terrible effects often produced by smallpox on these mountain folk gave him the idea of visiting them and taking up the profession of inoculator, after he had taken some lessons in the hospitals. Now he has been practising with success for thirty or forty years, but all he makes by way of income is not more than thirty or forty pounds sterling per annum. It cannot be denied that this man is really useful to society, and I believe him to be worthy of the attention of the Government, who might give him a small pension by way of recompense for past efforts and for encouragement to continue them.

When he had told me his whole story he naturally wished to know mine. 'Pray, Sir,' said he, 'what do you follow yourself?' 'You perceive,' I answered, 'I follow the road.' Tapping me on the shoulder he said, 'You take me short.' It was a new idea for him, perhaps, that a stranger's affairs are his own affair.

After this little story, can people take for truth the tales which represent the common folk of Ireland as idle, stupid, and incapable of improvement, when people reputed more clever have refused up to the present to adopt the sanitary practice of inoculation? On the Continent, not only would the peasants refuse to allow their children to be inoculated, but even people comfortably off would make a like refusal. In England well-meaning proprietors are often obliged to beg the parents to submit; in Scotland they have not yet succeeded in securing adoption of the method, and yet it is generally adopted in Ireland even in its wildest parts. The children are not in any way specially cared for; they run about and amuse themselves, nearly naked, after inoculation as before. When the fever takes them, it is only then that the inoculator is called to see them, when he administers a few simple remedies, which, pardonably, he may make somewhat mysterious in order to increase his credit, and to prevent the parents from becoming accustomed to apply these remedies themselves – a procedure which would mean to him the loss of his daily bread.

DE LATOCHAYE, *A Frenchman's Walk Through Ireland*

THE FIELD

This is a parish in which you understand hunger. But there are many hungers. There is a hunger for food – a natural hunger. There is the hunger of the flesh – a natural understandable hunger. There is a hunger for home, for love, for children. These things are good – they are good because they are necessary. But there is also the hunger for land. And in this parish, you, and your fathers before you knew what it was to starve because you did not own your own land – and that has increased; this unappeasable hunger for land. But how far are you prepared to go to satisfy this hunger. Are you prepared to go to the point of robbery? Are you prepared to go to the point of murder? Are you prepared to kill for land? Was this man killed for land? Did he give his life's blood for a field?

JOHN B. KEANE, Part of the Bishop's speech from *The Field*

A PAGAN PLACE

Your father met your mother at that dance but didn't throw two words to her. Your mother was all dolled up, home from America on holiday, had a long dress and peroxide in her hair. Your mother put the eye on him then and got her brother to invite him up to their house to walk the land.

Your father could guess the acreage of any field by walking it. That and horses was his hobby and off nights with Dan Egan for sing-songs and out on the lake shooting duck. Dan Egan and he lived in a big house with an old tiddly nanny and when they got home drunk in the mornings she used to bring up shaving water and whiskey, a mug of each. Kept a roaring fire they did in one room and in all the other rooms there were bats, and mice, and dark pieces of furniture.

Your father was an orphan but his old tiddly nanny took care of him and when he wanted shaving water or a headache powder all he had to do was press a bell and when the green gong trembled in the kitchen his old tiddly nanny said Bad cess to you but went to him all the same.

EDNA O'BRIEN, *A Pagan Place*

Sorcerer got his hind legs under him, and hardened his crest against the bit, as we all hustled along the drive after the flying figure of my wife. I knew very little about horses, but I realized that even with the hounds tumbling hysterically out of the covert, Sorcerer comported himself with the manners of the best society. Up a side road I saw Flurry Knox opening half of a gate and cramming through it; in a moment we also had crammed through, and the turf of a pasture field was under our feet. Dr Hickey leaned forward and took hold of his horse; I did likewise, with the trifling difference that my horse took hold of me, and I steered for Flurry Knox with single-hearted purpose, the hounds, already a field ahead, being merely an exciting and noisy accompaniment of this endeavour. A heavy stone wall was the first occurrence of note. Flurry chose a place where the top was loose, and his clumsy-looking brown mare changed feet on the rattling stones like a fairy. Sorcerer came at it, tense and collected as a bow at full stretch, and sailed steeply into the air; I saw the wall far beneath me, with an unsuspected ditch on the far side, and I felt my hat following me at the full stretch of its guard as we swept over it, then, with a long slant, we descended to earth some sixteen feet from where we had left it, and I was possessor of the gratifying fact that I had achieved a good-sized 'fly', and had not perceptibly moved in my saddle. Subsequent disillusioning experience has taught me that but few horses jump like Sorcerer, so gallantly, so sympathetically, and with such supreme mastery of the subject; but none the less the enthusiasm that he imparted to me has never been extinguished, and that October morning ride revealed to me the unsuspected intoxication of fox-hunting.

SOMERVILLE AND ROSS, *Experiences of an Irish RM*

SONG FOR A CORNCRAKE

Why weave rhetoric on your voice's loom,
Shuttling at the bottom of my garden
In meadowsweet and broom?
Crepuscular, archaic politician,
It's time to duck down,
Little bridegroom.

Why draft an epic on a myth of doom
In staunchly nailed iambics
Launched nightly near my room?
Since all you need to say is *crex*
Give us lyrics,
Little bridegroom.

Why go on chiselling mottoes for a tomb,
Counting on a scythe to spare
Your small defenceless home?
Quicken your tune, O improvise, before
The combine and the digger come,
Little bridegroom.

RICHARD MURPHY, *High Island*

TWILIGHT

White mists were beginning to rise in the low marshy ground
between these hills and the townland of Castle Kevin, and I
could hear dogs barking through it and geese cackling on the
bog. A lane runs round the valley to join the road to Laragh,
and the few cottages along it were sending up blue lines of
smoke. Quite near me an old man was driving sheep down
from the hills through dense masses of purple heath.

What has given this vague but passionate anguish to the
twilights of Ireland? At this season particularly when the first
touch of autumn is felt in the evening air every cottage I pass
by among the mountains, with an unyoked donkey cart lying
[by] it and a hen going to roost on the three-legged pot beside
the door, or perhaps a pool with rushes round it and a few

children with the sadness of night coming upon them, makes me long that this twilight might be eternal and I pass these doors in endless pilgrimage. Yet they make me and, I believe, many or most people who feel these things, more dejected than any sight of misery.

At such moments one regrets every hour that one has lived outside Ireland and every night that one has passed in cities. Twilight and autumn are both full of the suggestion that we connect with death and the ending of earthly vigour, and perhaps in a country like Ireland this moment has an emphasis that is not known elsewhere. In another sense moments of supreme beauty and distinction make the impulses of the diurnal temperament jar against the impulses of the perpetual beauty which is hidden somewhere in the fountain from whence all life has come, and this jar leads us to the most profound and vain remorse anyone can experience.

J. M. SYNGE, *Prose Works*

THE FISHERMAN

Although I can see him still,
The freckled man who goes
To a grey place on a hill
In grey Connemara clothes
At dawn to cast his flies,
It's long since I began
To call up to the eyes
This wise and simple man.
All day I'd looked in the face
What I had hoped 'twould be
To write for my own race
And the reality;
The living men that I hate,
The dead man that I loved,
The craven man in his seat,
The insolent unreproved,
And no knave brought to book
Who has won a drunken cheer,
The witty man and his joke

Aimed at the commonest ear
The clever man who cries
The catch-cries of the clown,
The beating down of the wise
And great Art beaten down.

Maybe a twelvemonth since
Suddenly I began,
In scorn of this audience,
Imagining a man,
And his sun-freckled face,
And grey Connemara cloth,
Climbing up to a place
Where stone is dark under froth,
And the down-turn of his wrist
When the flies drop in the stream;
A man who does not exist,
A man who is but a dream;
And cried, 'Before I am old
I shall have written him one
Poem maybe as cold
And passionate as the dawn.'

W. B. YEATS, *Collected Poems*

It has always been said that the worst of all livings is to be made from the sea.

CONCHUR Ó SÍOCHAIN, *The Man from Cape Clear*

THE CLADDAGH

The inhabitants of the 'Claddagh' are a colony of fishermen, and they number, with their families, between five and six thousand. Their market-place adjoins one of the old gates of the town, and is close to the remains of a fortified tower. Here they sell their fish, but it is apart from their own dominion –

'their own dominion' it may be called literally, for they are governed by their own king and their own laws: and it is difficult, if not impossible, to make them obedient to any other.

The Claddagh is a populous district lying to the right of the harbour, consisting of streets, squares, and lanes; all inhabited by fishermen. They claim the right to exercise complete and exclusive control over the bay, and, indeed, over all the bays of the county. They are peaceable and industrious, and their cottages are cleaner and better furnished than those of most of the Galway dwellings; but if any of the 'rights' they have enjoyed for centuries are infringed, they become so violent that nothing can withstand them.

This singular community are still governed by a 'king' elected annually, and a number of bye-laws of their own; at one time this king was absolute – as powerful as a veritable despot; but his power has yielded, like all despotic powers, to the times, and now he is, as one of his subjects informed us, 'nothing more than the Lord Mayor of Dublin or any other city'. He has still, however, much influence, and sacrifices himself, literally without fee or reward, for 'the good of the people'; he is constantly occupied hearing and deciding causes and quarrels, for his people never by any chance appeal to a higher tribunal. In the Claddagh, too, there are many remarkable remains of those singular antiquities which prevail in the town.

Their king is indeed completely one of themselves; his rank and station being only indicated, according to Mr Hardiman, by a white sail and colours flying from the mast-head of his boat, when at sea – where he acts as 'admiral'. They have many peculiar customs: one is worthy of especial note. The wedding ring is a heir-loom in a family. It is regularly transferred by the mother to her daughter first married; and so on to their descendants. These rings are large, of solid gold, and not unfrequently cost from two to three pounds each. The people are, in general, comfortably clad; and their houses are, for the most part, neatly furnished. We entered several of them, and among others, that of the ruler of the district. His majesty, however, was at sea; but we were introduced to his royal family – a group of children and grandchildren, who for ruddy health might have been coveted by any veritable

monarch of Christendom . . . Taken altogether, this primitive
suburb included, there is no town in Ireland so interesting as
Galway.

MR AND MRS HALL, *Ireland: Scenery and Character*
1825–40

A WHIRLPOOL OF THE SEA THAT SWALLOWS SHIPS

Not far to the north from the islands of which we have been
speaking is a certain wonderful whirlpool in the sea. All the
waves of the sea from all parts, even those remote, flow and
strike together here as if by agreement. They seem to pour
themselves into the secret recesses of nature here, and are, so
to speak, devoured in the abyss. If a ship happens to touch it,
it is caught and pulled with such violence of the waves that
the force of the pull downwards immediately swallows it up
for ever.

GIRALDUS CAMBRENSIS, *History and Topography of*
Ireland (Trans. John O'Meara)

THE CLEGGAN DISASTER

Even during the finest weather there is danger of sudden
storms. Not many years ago, on 'the calmest night of the week,'
a gale hit the fishing boats, and few of them reached land.
Forty-four men lost their lives. Pat Concannon, on Bofin, still
has the marks on his hands of the rope that he held for seven
hours that night, the rope that, fastened to his net as a sea-
anchor, kept the head of his boat to the wind. There had been
a warning on the wireless from Daventry, but it had been
missed on the island. Local weather experts saw no sign of
coming storm. Only one incident gave cause for anxiety. A
few nights earlier a phantom ship had been seen. It had followed the boats all through the night. It had made no answer
to any of the hails from the boats. This the men took as a
warning. But they could not give up their means of livelihood.

The night of the storm there were boats from Cleggan and Rossadilisk on the mainland fishing with those from Bofin. The gale came on them suddenly, so suddenly that there was no time to cut away the nets. In the darkness men still in the boats could hear the shouts of their friends drowning. One man saw his brother go down within an oar's length of him but could do nothing to help.

For seven hours Pat held the rope, his knees wedged against the stem post of the boat. Up each wave he had to haul her lest she should broach to, then he would slack away the rope to let her down the other side. Occasionally he would shout orders to the younger members of the crew. All the time the sea was rising, angered by the ebb-tide against the wind. The blow had started at seven o'clock in the evening. By two o'clock in the morning they had drifted nine miles, and now they were in danger of running on the breakers off High Island. But the wind had begun to drop, so they cut their nets and made for Cleggan. It took them two hours of desperate rowing to get there. When they reached land they found the bodies of many of their friends already washed ashore, some of them tangled in their own nets.

It is the custom in the west, when the men are fishing, for the women of the house either to stay awake in bed or to remain dressed about the house in order to keep the fire going. That night nobody on shore had lain down. When Pat Concannon and his crew landed Pat walked up to the house of a friend. 'Good night, Mrs King,' he said.

'Good night, Pat,' she said. 'What has you here at this hour of the night?' 'I was waiting round,' he said, 'and I thought I'd come in and sit down by the fire.' Mrs King made him a cup of tea. Later the doctor came and dressed his hands. Nothing more was said. 'The grief was too great.'

ROBERT GIBBINGS, *Lovely is the Lee*

THE SEAL

The little bay ringed round with broken cliffs
Gathers the tide-borne wrack,
And there the islanders come day by day
For weed that shall enrich their barren fields.
Here, since the cliff-path gaped,
Cloven by the winter's wrecking storms,
They had gathered to remake the shattered way.
We idled as they laboured
With listless, laughing talk of that and this,
When suddenly a seal,
Rising and falling on the changing tide,
Lifted a dripping face and looked at us,
A mournful face, more sad
Than the grey sadness of a moonlit wave.
We spoke, and in a moment it was gone,
And an unpeopled sea
Washed up and died in foam upon the shore.
Said one: 'He's lonely after his brother still.'
And so we heard the story,
A mournful memory of the Island, cherished
By the old dreaming people,
And told round the dim fire on winter nights.
One twilight of late spring
The men had killed a seal out on the beaches
And brought it to a sea-cave for the skinning,
And, as they worked red-handed,
A voice out of the sea called 'Brother!' once,
And then 'Brother!' again. Then silence, only
A wind that sighed on the unquiet sea.
So standing in the surf
They saw as now a seal rising and falling
On a slow swinging sea.
They lifted their red hands and he was gone
Silently slipping into a silent wave.

ROBIN FLOWER, *The Western Island*

HUNTING LODGE

At the bottom of a narrow creek you must imagine 'a low, snug dwelling, and in good repair'. The foam of the Atlantic breaks sometimes against the windows, while a huge cliff, seaward, defends it from the storm, and, on the land side, a sudden hill shelters it from the north wind. The bent roof is impervious to the rain; the rooms are neat, well arranged, and comfortable. In the parlour, if the evening be chilly, a turf fire sparkles on the hearth; and when dried bog-deal is added to the embers, it emits a fragrant and delightful glow, superseding the necessity of candles. The long and measured swell of the Atlantic would almost lull a troubled conscience to repose; and that rural hum, which attends upon the farmyard, rouses the refreshed sleeper in the morning. In the calm of evening I hear the shrill cry of the sand-lark; and in the early dawn, the crowing of the cock grouse. I see the salmon fling themselves over the smooth tide, as they hurry from the sea to re-ascend their native river. And while I drink claret that never paid the revenue a farthing, or indulge over that proscribed beverage – the produce and the scourge of this wild district – I trace from the window the outline of a range of hills, where the original red-deer of Ireland are still existing – none of your park-fed venison, that tame, spiritless, diminutive, which a boy may assassinate with his 'birding-piece', but the remnant of that noble stock, which hunters of other days, *O'Connor the Cus Dhu* and *Cormac Bawn Mac Tavish*, once delighted in pursuing.

The offices of this wild dwelling are well adapted to the edifice. In winter the ponies have their stable, and kine and sheep a comfortable shed. Nor are the dogs forgotten; for them a warm and sheltered kennel is fitted up with benches, and well provided with straw. Many a sporting-lodge in England, on which thousands have been expended, lacks the comforts of my kinsman's unpretending cottage. Where are the coachhouses? Those, indeed, would be useless appendages; for the nearest road on which a wheel could turn is ten miles distant from the lodge.

W. H. MAXWELL, *Wild Sports of the West*

71

A LONELY BUSINESS

Ireland, especially the South, is an infinitely mysterious country; one is never quite alone, although one seems to be so; there is always someone watching or listening behind a hedge or in a doorway. There is tremendous politeness and gaiety, juxtaposed to sullenness and suspicion; I have never found, though, a more entirely congenial surrounding in my life. Cork itself is an entirely Continental seaport; quite unlike anything English; built upon four or five tongues of the river Lea, with eighteenth-century wharves and quays and warehouses, and then little hovels and cottages and lanes all up the hills behind the town. Desmond and I walked each night till nearly two o'clock, talking, up and down these steep ancient alleys and bye-streets and once we heard people singing inside one of the cottages, something about the green Land of Ireland, and stood outside in the moonlight and listened for half an hour.

JAMES POPE HENNESSY, *Letters*

CORK

It was a hot, sunny day. The wheels of a donkey cart had parted company in the main street of Cork. The sun poured down on a laughing, animated crowd that would not have seemed out of place in Seville.

I know no other country which sees such humour in the, at times, almost evil intractability of inanimate objects. In England a breakdown in the road is a shameful spectacle. It reflects discredit on the person involved. It is inefficient. The debris is at once rushed to the side and the business of life sweeps on. In England a breakdown is a matter of anger; in Ireland for laughter. This argues a different philosophy of life. Perhaps only nations with a profound spiritual attitude to life can laugh at the occasional failure of material affairs. Or perhaps that is the reflection of a mind becoming tuned-in to the subtlety of Ireland; for no man can live for even a week in Ireland, as in Spain, without looking for a religious explanation to any peculiarity.

Cork was the most foreign city I had seen in Ireland – foreign not in appearance but in atmosphere. One was surprised to hear the crowds talking a high-pitched English. I felt that on a summer's day Cork should be full of vivid, striped umbrellas, beneath which the visitor might sit in the shade and sip grenadine.

It was in 1920 that at the height of the madness of the 'Trouble' half Cork was burnt down. I felt sorry that Cork has not taken advantage of this disaster to rebuild its streets in a fashion more in keeping with the distinctive character of its people.

Cork is the capital of Munster: if anything should happen to Dublin it would be, obviously, the capital of the Free State. It is built on an island in the centre of the River Lee. A man, who should have known better, told me that it gets its name because it floats like a cork on the water. Cork, however, is derived from an Irish word meaning marsh.

There is a legend in Ireland to the effect that a Cork man can make a fortune where any other man would be applying for outdoor relief. It is certainly true that the people of Cork are different from the people in other parts of Ireland. They have a tradition as aristocratic as that of Dublin. They are clannish. For centuries they intermarried within their own walls, so that a family feeling exists between all men of Cork, which explains why when a Cork man takes over a business, say in Dublin, other men of Cork appear as if by magic in the firm.

Brilliant conversation began in Cork during the eighteenth century, and it is still going on. It is carried on in a quick, high-pitched, musical Welsh accent. (Or have the Welsh a Cork accent?)

They stay up so late in Cork making epigrams that the shops do not open until 9.30 to 10 am.

Through the wide streets of Cork, and beside the fine quays, moves a crowd just a pace quicker than any other Irish crowd.

H. V. MORTON, *In Search of Ireland*

CORK

That is a confusing city, of which Irishmen everywhere who do not come from Cork profess to be afraid. And it is a fact that while it reclines there between the arms of the River Lee, looking beautiful and a little raffish and a little tired, as though it had too many things to remember, it is also a volcano of energy spouting out people who go out and take over great tracts of government and industry in Dublin, Pittsburgh and Sydney.

CLAUD COCKBURN, *I, Claud*

DUBLIN

Strumpet city in the sunset
Suckling the bastard brats of Scots, of Englishry, of Huguenot.
Brave sons breaking from the womb, wild sons fleeing from
   their Mother.
Wilful city of savage dreamers.
So old, so sick with memories!
Old Mother
Some they say are damned,
But you, I know, will walk the streets of Paradise
Head high, and unashamed.

DENIS JOHNSTON, *The Old Lady Says 'No'*

DUBLIN SUBURBS

My way led through Stephen's Green, and the long decay of Dublin that began with the Union engaged my thoughts, and I fared sighing for the old-time mansions that had been turned into colleges and presbyteries. There were lodging-houses in Harcourt Street, and beyond Harcourt Street the town dwindled, first into small shops, then into shabby-genteel villas; at Terenure, I was among cottages, and within sight of purple hills, and when the Dodder was crossed, at the end of the village street, a great wall began, high as a prison wall; it might well have been mistaken for one, but the trees told it was a park wall, and the great ornamental gateway was a pleasant object. It came into sight suddenly – a great pointed edifice finely designed, and after admiring it I wandered on, crossing an old grey bridge. The Dodder again, I said. And the beautiful green country unfolded, a little melancholy for lack of light and shade, for lack, I added, of a ray to gild the fields. A beautiful country falling into ruin. The beauty of neglect – yet there is none in thrift. My eyes followed the long herds wandering knee-deep in succulent herbage, and I remembered that every other country I had seen was spoilt more or less by human beings, but this country was nearly empty, only an occasional herdsman to remind me of myself in this drift of ruined suburb, with a wistful line of mountains enclosing it, and one road curving among the hills, and everywhere high walls – parks, in the centre of which stand stately eighteenth-century mansions.

GEORGE MOORE, *Hail and Farewell*

BACK TO DUBLIN

The streets bristle with danger. You may be mooching along, intending no harm to a soul, at peace with heaven and earth. Towards you comes a lank figure in hairy tweeds and battered hat, one of Dublin's innumerable geniuses. From the air of purpose in his bearing it is clear that he means to borrow a pound. In many places the loan of a pound will purchase immunity not only from further applications but from the society of the borrower too and may thus be regarded as a prudent investment; but in Dublin it has the strange power of creating a bond between the parties that nothing seems able to shake. Jesus, that old pound! if I hadn't forgotten every word about it! would j'ever make it two, till next Friday? Once again Operation Snowball commences.

Here, then, a borrowing genius comes and just in time you pull up, slap your forehead histrionically as if remembering the milk on the stove, wheel about and make down a side-turning as fast as your legs will carry you. A tall, distinguished man coming out of a shop raises his hat and looks daggers. Up to that moment you were not conscious of having offended in any way, had cherished indeed the belief that you were rather a favourite, but no sooner do you get that steely look than you realize what is behind it. It flashes across your mind that when you were last in Dublin you never went to see this person. True, in order to do so you would first have taken the train: and then the bus: and the trains and buses are dovetailed brilliantly to miss each other: and then you would have climbed up half a mountain, the last stretch over rock: and it was pouring with rain every day. You have only to look at the curl of that long, thin nostril, the sit of that head on the shoulders, however, to see how inadequate the excuse would be.

'Good morning! I'm back again,' you quaver.

'Welcome. I had begun to think you were dead,' and he passes on.

HONOR TRACY, *Mind You, I've Said Nothing!*

DUBLIN

The natural surroundings and architectural layout of Dublin also had their influence on the personality of the people. Dublin is a city, as George Moore said pleasantly about it, 'wandering between hill and sea'. In the Dubliner's mind is the knowledge that he can always get to sandy beaches, or goat-paths in lonely hills in less than a half-hour. Dublin Bay with its long beaches stretches for almost forty miles, and behind it lies a crescent of hills each merging into one another, with soft names like Kilmashogue, the Feather Bed, the Sally Gap, the Silver Spears.

The architects who laid the city out in the eighteenth century were always conscious of the natural beauty surrounding it. They crowned their public buildings with green domes to merge with the sky and the tidal waters of the Liffey. Between the tall houses and wide streets they framed panoramas of the hills, so that on clear days vistas of green and gold strike the eye at the end of a street or square. They bent stone until it accommodated the clouds and knew exactly how to use hill and sky against an urban background.

ULICK O'CONNOR, *Oliver St John Gogarty: A Poet and His Times*

CAPPAGHGLASS

Cappaghglass is a port and market town in the west of Ireland set in spectacular surroundings – a range of jagged blue mountains behind, the sea in front, with a couple of islands and the lighthouse. It is a place that is a lot more beautiful for its setting than for its architecture. A bird's-eye view would show a string of grey roofs cut by the river and dominated by the two churches and the old people's home. The core of the town is the line of Victorian houses and shops running along either side of the main street before it debouches into the market square. On the south side of the square is the harbour and jetty, behind which stood the old station where the emigrant said his last farewell and from where the cattle were shipped eastward and the barrels of salted fish were dispatched to America.

The two churches stand to east and west of the town like bookends. The Catholic church is the enormous Victorian Gothic edifice; the Protestant church, an earlier Gothic shoebox with a tower, is a lot smaller and shabbier, and, to most tastes, prettier. The steady increase of population to over six thousand during the last decade is reflected by the brand new suburbs that have risen to the west. Council housing is mixed with determinedly prosperous bungalows laid out with tarmacadamed drives, landscaped gardens and plastic urns and ornaments. At the east approach a sad little factory is empty and boarded up. Along the coast where the view is best a thin line of bungalows looks out to sea. Among them is the odd farmhouse, sometimes converted into a comfortable holiday home, sometimes still the home of the small farmer who has sold his land. New Zealand flax and escallonia hedging try to shelter the gardens from the sea wind.

Back in the main street, built for horse traffic, the tractors and lorries laden with supermarket goods try to squeeze between the cars half-parked on the pavement on both sides of the street. You can catch a whiff of the past as you stare at the three-storey houses with their lace-curtained Gothic windows, the ruinously big hotel, and the solid bank building, which all recall an age when the street was dust or mud. It is easy to screw up your eyes and imagine 'the appearance of poverty and desertion' described by a nineteenth-century traveller where 'even in well-built and substantial houses every second pane of glass has given way to a board nailed across the window, or a still more offensive paper patching. Bricks or stones or tiles, as they fall from the piles of buildings, which really would constitute a handsome range, if in repair, are suffered to remain where fortune may place them, till the wheels of the heavy carts crush them under the dust which no munificent law controls . . .' That description dates from before the famine. But memories of poverty are a lot more recent, and evident not only in photographs of scenes of forty and fifty years ago where you can see women in shawls, barefoot children and men in raincoats standing with their cattle before the pillared shopfronts. The testimony of old people brings these scenes vividly to life.

Up to twenty years ago Cappaghglass had regular fairs, men and animals thrown together in rowdy chaos beneath the Celtic cross and its list of patriots. The town and country people were set in the old ways, the town an intimate place where crafts and traditional skills flourished – blacksmiths, harness makers, tailors, and all the cobblers making stout hobnailed boots. The few survivors who practise these trades are old men who recall how skills and secrets were passed from father to son until the coming of mass production. You can sometimes come across an old cobbler or harness maker in his shop somewhere in the ramshackle network of old streets and lanes behind the main square.

The gloomy atmospheric old pubs and shops have smartened up. Until the late 'fifties the main store was like an Aladdin's cave, selling everything from sausage to pieces of rope, from underwear to tickets to America. Boots and mackintoshes hung from the wooden ceiling and bolted cash cups ran with your change to the cashier who was sitting in a sort of signal box in the middle. Such trappings have been replaced by super-market shelves and a delicatessen counter. The old shopfronts, divided up by slender arches, have been exchanged for plate glass stuck with information about baked beans and biscuits, and the black and gilt lettering above has changed to crisper capitals and logos.

PETER SOMERVILLE-LARGE, *Cappaghglass*

HOME TOWN

Squeezed between the estuary of the Blackwater River and the steep hill behind, squeezed too – harshly so – by human decisions of more recent vintage, the town of Youghal, in County Cork, Ireland, advertises as succinctly as you might wish the facts of life in a poor country in the middle of this decade. There's no need to go below the fiftieth parallel to encounter what are often sedately described as 'problems of underdevelopment'.

It's not as though each time I go home there the place hastens to disclose the changes in its fortunes. Seen in the pale morning light from across the river, the quays and gray stone houses surely look much as they did to Sir Walter Raleigh, who was mayor of Youghal in 1588; to Cromwell, who made the town the base for his rampages in 1650; to Michael Collins, who sheltered near there during the Civil War of 1922. From the middle distance, at least, Irish towns like Youghal do not conspicuously display the fingerprints of change, which is no doubt why John Huston and his film crew settled in Youghal for a few uproarious months in 1954 to re-create Melville's New Bedford for the film *Moby Dick*.

A thirty-five-year-old photograph of North Main Street looks very much like a seventy-five-year-old one of the same view, to either side of the great Clock Gate. When I was driven to parochial school in a trap in 1948, I can remember horse-drawn transportation outnumbered automobiles ten to one and knots of unemployed men lounged away their days in front of Farrell's grain store. But by the early 1960s the carts and traps were mostly gone and a prosperous Youghal was forced to import labour from the surrounding countryside. Amid the increasing (but still modest) affluence of Youghal's population of five thousand the town council faced a parking problem, and the odd BMW and even Mercedes announced the spending power and great expectations of a growing managerial class.

Today, a drive down North Main Street suggests that Youghal remains an emblem of this post-war boom, which, for Ireland, surged in the 1960s.

Just for an instant at the turn of this year Youghal seemed unchanged from those glory days. Home from abroad to visit the old place and the old folk, one is loath to dwell upon intimations of mortality creeping across the features of one's parents or one's town. But after a day I knew well enough that even if the three new little high-tech plants on the edge of town represented a reversal of the desperate crisis of four years ago, the situation was still pretty bad. 'Youghal's fighting back,' the locals said to me each day, but from the anxious way they put it I knew that for a time the place had been lying awfully still on the floor.

ALEXANDER COCKBURN, *Corruptions of Empire*

LIMERICK

Limerick – as the famous John Mahaffy, the Trinity College wit, used to say – was the only city in Western Europe where you could see a bittern standing undisturbed in the main street at half past nine in the morning.

V. S. PRITCHETT, *At Home and Abroad*

A PRECIOUS POSSESSION

It is hard to go far anywhere in this country without meeting some person of real psychological or pictorial interest. The other day near Ballyduff I met one of the most delightful old women that I have yet fallen in with. She was coming along with a bottle of milk in one hand and a bundle of some sort in the other. When I got near she set down her bundle and looked at me with a little rogue-like smile.

'Have you any money?' she asked when I was opposite her. I told [her] I might find some about me.

'Well,' she said, 'I am very poor.' I told [her] I was poorer than she was because she had a bottle of milk and I had none. She pulled the cork out of her bottle and handed it to me.

'Take a sup,' she said, 'maybe you're drouthy with walking in the sun.' She wore her hair, which was still a warm tint, in a great bush on her shoulders, and her little face had wrinkled up to a dimpled humorous pose, that is quite unique in this country. [One could no more] meet or talk to this old woman without smiling a little [than] one could look sternly at a rollicking, quizzical infant.

We were both too weary to talk for very long, and I was soon on my way again. At the next turn in the road near Laragh I came on a tinkers' camp in a fragment of a wood that grows at the apex of the meeting between the Annamoe river and the waters from Glendalough and Lough Nahanagan. Dusk was coming on rapidly yet no one seemed to be at the camp but two young children that I could see through a gate sitting up with the light of the fire full on their faces. They were singing a few bars of some droning song over and over again, that I could just hear above the noise of the two rivers and the waving of the black fir trees that stood above them.

People like these, like the old woman and these two beautiful children, are a precious possession for any country. They console us, one moment at least, for the manifold and beautiful life we have all missed who have been born in modern Europe . . .

J. M. SYNGE, *Prose Works*

WHAT IS AN IRISHMAN?

When I say that I am an Irishman I mean that I was born in Ireland, and that my native language is the English of Swift and not the unspeakable jargon of the mid-XIX century London newspapers. My extraction is the extraction of most Englishmen: that is, I have no trace in me of the commercially imported North Spanish strain which passes for aboriginal Irish: I am a genuine typical Irishman of the Danish, Norman, Cromwellian, and (of course) Scotch invasions. I am violently and arrogantly Protestant by family tradition; but let no English Government therefore count on my allegiance: I am English enough to be an inveterate Republican and Home Ruler. It is true that one of my grandfathers was an Orangeman; but then his sister was an abbess; and his uncle, I am proud to say, was hanged as a rebel.

GEORGE BERNARD SHAW, Introduction to *John Bull's Other Island*

ACCOMPLISHMENTS OF AN IRISHMAN

To smoke his dudheen,
To drink his cruiskeen,
To flourish his alpeen,
To wallop a spalpeen.
P. W. JOYCE, *English As We Speak It In Ireland*

It was altogether a very jolly life that I led in Ireland. I was always moving about, and soon found myself to be in pecuniary circumstances which were opulent in comparison with those of my past life. The Irish people did not murder me, nor did they even break my head. I soon found them to be good-humoured, clever – the working classes very much more intelligent than those of England – economical, and hospitable. We hear much of their spendthrift nature; but extravagance is not the nature of an Irishman. He will count the shillings in a pound much more accurately than an Englishman, and will with much more certainty get twelve pennyworth from

each. But they are perverse, irrational, and but little bound by
the love of truth.

ANTHONY TROLLOPE, *Autobiography*

The Irish love failure. In their folklore success is inexcusable,
but the fumbled ball, the lost promotion, the one drink too
many are to them the stuff of romance: they turn the winner's
laurels into a salad for the loser to eat, adding clichés for
seasoning.

HUGH LEONARD, *Home Before Night*

I used to sit on a wall with an old peasant in the mountainy
country near Clifden while he let his greyhound off to put up
a hare. If it came off, he would be shouting with excitement:
'He has him! He has *not*! He has him! He has *not*! He has him
beat. He has him destroyed in the corner. He has *not*, he's
away over the wall.' And so on. An afternoon came pelting to
life for a poor man living alone with his rags, his whiskey
bottle and his dog.

V. S. PRITCHETT, *At Home and Abroad*

MADNESS IN THE COUNTRY

JIMMY *entirely convinced*: It's a fright surely. I knew a party was
kicked in the head by a red mare, and he went killing horses
a great while, till he eat the insides of a clock and died after.

J. M. SYNGE, *Playboy of the Western World*

KITCHENS

The difference of the English and Irish character is nowhere
more plainly discerned than in their respective kitchens. With
the former, this apartment is probably the cleanest, and certainly the most orderly, in the house. It is rarely intruded

into by those unconnected, in some way, with its business. Everything it contains is under the vigilant eye of its chief occupant, who would imagine it quite impossible to carry on her business, whether of an humble or important nature, if her apparatus was subjected to the hands of the unauthorised. An Irish kitchen is devoted to hospitality in every sense of the word. Its doors are open to almost all loungers and idlers; and the chances are that Billy Bawn, the cripple, or Judy Molloy, the deaf old hag, are more likely to know where to find the required utensil than the cook herself. It is usually a temple dedicated to the goddess of disorder; and, too often joined with her, is the potent deity of dirt. It is not that things are out of their place, for they have no place. It isn't that the floor is not scoured, for you cannot scour dry mud into anything but wet mud. It isn't that the chairs and tables look filthy, for there are none. It isn't that the pots, and plates, and pans don't shine, for you see none to shine. All you see is a grimy, black ceiling, an uneven clay floor, a small darkened window, one or two unearthly-looking recesses, a heap of potatoes in the corner, a pile of turf against the wall, two pigs and a dog under the single dresser, three or four chickens on the window-sill, an old cock moaning on the top of a rickety press, and a crowd of ragged garments, squatting, standing, kneeling, and crouching, round the fire, from which issues a babel of strange tongues, not one word of which is at first intelligible to ears unaccustomed to such eloquence.

ANTHONY TROLLOPE, *The Kellys and the O'Kellys*

DE QUINCEY

I was standing outside a hardware shop noting the different local patterns of spades, some with a single step, some 'eared' on both sides, some with straight sides, some tapering, when a woman said to me: 'Have you ever read De Quincey? Hasn't he the wonderful English? My husband is inside buying rat traps.'

ROBERT GIBBINGS, *Lovely is the Lee*

Apart from the lulling climate of the lovely Blackwater valley, there are other factors which sometimes seem to make writing in the country more arduous, more of a strain on the brain and emotions than in the city. What it amounts to is that part of the time the writer in the country is subjected to a series of interruptions – like alarms of foot-and-mouth disease, fences falling down, or a catastrophic drop in the market price of turkeys – which in the city do not impinge. From these, it is true, I was to a very large extent protected by Patricia who, in addition to being an expert with horses and turning a wilderness of scutch grass into a garden a whole family could live on, took other farm problems, of which she had no previous knowledge, in her stride.

But when you have shaken off those problems of life in the country, or rather have handed them to someone else, you are sitting there thinking, and your skin creeps slightly with the sensation that there is absolutely nothing between you and eternity – not some eternity in the future, but all round and behind you. You have the feeling you had as a child when nobody would tell you what there was beyond the place where outer space ended. A simple sensation, but eerie, too.

In our part of Ireland the sensation was heightened for me by the awareness one continuously had there of what may be called the presence of the past. There are, of course, innumerable places where what are called 'antiquities' are as numerous as here. But even in, say, Rome the past seems to me to be keeping its distance, and allowing itself to be judged and studied with a certain detachment. Here in the country it is not so. In the stony circle of the Druid wood at Blarney – a place which perhaps was sacred even before the Druids adopted it – you are tumbled, almost as though you had been physically pushed, head over heels into pre-history. The trees there, forming the grove in which is situated the ring of sacred stones, have been demonstrated by arboreal experts to be older than any other trees in the world, with the exception of the Californian redwoods. The grove, and the stones – the fact that this was a sacred place thousands of years ago – are, one can hardly doubt, the true explanation of the legend of the

Blarney stone. Every century has had a different account of the origin of the belief in the stone's magical powers – explanations which are mystical, religious or matter-of-factually political according to the prevailing climate of thought. But there would have been no legend about the stone's powers if it were not associated with a holy place, though nobody knows what first made it holy nor how distant, primitive and furry were the first worshippers.

Across one of our fields runs the outline of a rath – a line of underground dwellings built, probably, as a fortification and defence against early Scandinavian invaders. They, too, had to abandon airier ways of living and take to the underground shelters, and they seem very close.

This lurking and sometimes intrusive presence of the past might perhaps be supposed to weaken or dull the impact of the present. The contrary is the case. This crowding in of history serves instead to intensify a consciousness of the pressures and contradictions of life and society in the present.

CLAUD COCKBURN, I, Claud

SOME PEOPLE

We were greatly helped in all our perplexities by Sean O'Faolain, the first editor of the magazine, whose literary judgement and wise counsel were always at its disposal. Sean stands out in Dublin like a rock in foaming seas. In appearance he is like some respectable English burgher, tall and spare, rosy and blue-eyed; he pulls on a pipe in a calm English way and speaks in a manner imperturbable as it is urbane. He possesses moreover an integrity which is entirely alien to the Irish genius; and his mere presence soothes and reassures. Under it all he is as dotty as they come. He suffers intermittently from violent rushes of blood to the head which bear fruit in the shape of resounding letters to the *Irish Times*; and I understand that for every one of them that he posts, ten are written and torn up. Perfectly aware that his adversaries are not worth the powder and shot, he falls to and peppers them with a will. On one occasion he proposed to sue a Bishop: and richly as that Bishop deserved to be sued and greatly as we all would have relished the proceedings, there can be no doubt but that it was the dream of a madman. Over the rest of us, however, he had always a wholesome and restraining influence.

HONOR TRACY, Mind You, I've Said Nothing!

GOVERNMENT HOUSE

Our next official appearance in Ireland was in Government House, Cork, a large and needlessly ugly villa on a hill-top, flanked by a screen wall, topped with bogus battlements. There was a flagstaff in front.

We were warned, as a General Commanding, my father represented the power if not the person of the Crown and was more important than he would have been in the same rank in England. Much impressed, my mother bought a poodle.

We arrived just before the hunting season opened and my parents busily concerned themselves collecting some mounts, two of which could also draw the official carriage. The dual purpose steeds had breeding and showed it when driving on the steep hill upon which Government House was perched. There came the day when Lady Aberdeen visited the city and, buttressed by two Bishops and every doctor in Co. Cork, addressed a meeting on Tuberculosis. It lasted two hours over time on a cold day. Apart from her own frozen feet, my mother became apprehensive. Our carriage was waiting outside to convey Her Excellency to luncheon. Their career up the corkscrew hill was even more staccato than she had feared. As her large and stately guest grew paler, my mother felt that her beloved horses must be excused. 'You see, Your Excellency, they are on *extra oats*. They are to be hunted to-morrow.' The stately guest paled still further.

NORA ROBERTSON, The Crowned Harp

AN ENGLISH GOTH

A gentleman in county Cavan had complained most bitterly of the injury done to him by some arrangement of the Post Office. The nature of his grievance has no present significance; but it was so unendurable that he had written many letters, couched in the strongest language. He was most irate, and indulged himself in that scorn which is so easy to an angry mind. The place was not in my district, but I was borrowed, being young and strong, that I might remember the edge of his personal wrath. It was mid-winter, and I drove up to his house, a squire's country seat, in the middle of a snow-storm, just as it was becoming dark. I was on an open jaunting-car, and was on my way from one little town to another, the cause of his complaint having reference to some mail conveyance between the two. I was certainly very cold, and very wet, and very uncomfortable when I entered his house. I was admitted by a butler, but the gentleman himself hurried into the hall. I at once began to explain my business. 'God bless me!' he said, 'you are wet through. John, get Mr Trollope some brandy and water – very hot.' I was beginning my story about the post again when he himself took off my greatcoat, and suggested that I should go up to my bedroom before I troubled myself with business. 'Bedroom!' I exclaimed. Then he assured me that he would not turn a dog out on such a night as that, and into a bedroom I was shown, having first drank the brandy and water standing at the drawing-room fire. When I came down I was introduced to his daughter, and the three of us went into dinner. I shall never forget his righteous indignation when I again brought up the postal question on the departure of the young lady. Was I such a Goth as to contaminate wine with business? So I drank my wine, and then heard the young lady sing while her father slept in his armchair. I spent a very pleasant evening, but my host was too sleepy to hear anything about the Post Office that night. It was absolutely necessary that I should go away the next morning after breakfast, and I explained that the matter must be discussed then. He shook his head and wrung his hands in unmistakable disgust – almost in despair. 'But what am I to say in my report?' I asked. 'Anything you please,' he said. 'Don't spare me, if you want an

excuse for yourself. Here I sit all the day, with nothing to do;
and I like writing letters.' I did report that Mr ―― was now
quite satisfied with the postal arrangement of his district; and
I felt a soft regret that I should have robbed my friend of his
occupation. Perhaps he was able to take up the Poor Law
Board, or to attack the Excise. At the Post Office nothing more
was heard from him.

ANTHONY TROLLOPE, Autobiography

EOIN 'POPE' O'MAHONY

There is still every year a commemorative service and a dinner
in Dublin for Eoin O'Mahony. He was known to everyone
from his schooldays onward as 'the Pope', but why this was
so no one knew. He was a great Irishman whose greatness lay
in a field that he had made peculiarly his own.

He had seen in the extended family a blueprint for what life
might one day be like. Perhaps some generations or centuries
from now groups of people, linked together maybe as kinsmen,
maybe as neighbours, will feel a special responsibility for each
other, based on a closer knowledge and affection than is possible in our faceless and centralized society. Eoin wanted to
restore richness and variety and friendship to lives that our
civilization had sterilized and, within the compass of one man's
powers, he succeeded.

I only attended one O'Mahony rally, but it had a wild spontaneity, a happy, confident chaos that must have had years of
practice, megatons of spiritual buoyancy, behind it. Only a
great artist in social intercourse could have brought it off.

Eoin had issued hundreds of gold-embossed invitations to
the O'Mahony rally at Dunmanus Castle in the name of the
Vicomte and Vicomtesse de O'Mahony, a nice young barrister
and his wife, who live at Orleans. The Vicomte was the elected
Chieftain of the Clan, and probably owed his election to Eoin,
who did not bother to tell him about the invitations.

A shower of them fell on Fleet Street and a reporter from
the Daily Express, attracted by the idea of an invitation from a
vicomtesse to dance in an ancient castle on a remote promon-
tory in West Cork (he swore that the word 'Dancing' was

written in the left-hand bottom corner), had packed his white tie and tails and, taking a day off his holidays and a ticket to Cork, had arrived at Dunmanus at the same time as ourselves. An English family with a tent and a caravan were encamped within the castle ruins and had just before been astounded by the arrival of an advance detachment of clansmen, bearing on long staves the banners of the O'Mahonys, and of all the nations that had given them refuge in the days of their exile.

They had planted their flags around the caravan, and very soon a thousand other O'Mahonys had followed them and the small alien encampment, amazed but entertained, had been politely and totally submerged. Soon Eoin was in the thick of it all, booming eloquently in three languages, kissing continental hands, explaining and introducing. The O'Mahony rank-and-file and their friends were then planted on one side of a broken-down moat and the Vicomte stood on the other with Eoin beside him to interpret.

'I have to apologize,' began the Vicomte in high good humour and in French, 'that this is not my castle, and that it has not any roof, and that we are not able to dance in it, and that it wasn't I sent out that invitation.' Eoin translated all this jovially, and then we quickly passed on to serious matters, the long history of the O'Mahonys of Carbery and Kinelmeaky, their kinship and rivalries with the O'Sullivans and MacCarthys. Only the journalist sulked. When there was a pause in the narrative, he went up to Eoin and said: 'I understood there was to be a dance.'

'Well,' said Eoin, 'there's an excellent hotel in Skibbereen. Very nice people indeed, and, if you tell them you want to dance, I am sure they'll be delighted.' Eoin was then swept away by his kinsmen, and the journalist went and sulked on a lump of fallen masonry. He grumbled to some bystanders that he had been brought to West Cork on false pretences, that this was his holiday, not a job. But soon he observed that the O'Mahonys were entertained rather than touched by his misadventure. They were pointing him out to each other – 'Do you see that fella? Did you hear what he has in his suitcase?' – and he saw that he was becoming a stock character in a new version of a traditional Irish story, the innocent Englishman, who had never heard of Pope O'Mahony.

So he moved off to Skibbereen and, drinking himself into a good humour in his hotel, wrote a charming account of the rally for the London daily.

That was a typical O'Mahony occasion. It was an everyday setting, the ruined castle, the rocky shore, the drifts of bog asphodel, the gorse, the pools of water lilies, white as well as orange. And there were everyday people there. There were solicitors from Cork and a garage proprietor from Killarney and hospital nurses and a camp counsellor from Massachusetts. More notable was Rev. Jeremiah O'Mahony from Palm Beach, who was President Kennedy's chaplain and pronounced his name O'Mahóney. The most surprising clansman from America was coal-black. Or could he have been like myself a mere O'Mahonyphile?

Without the magic of Pope O'Mahony to fuse us and transmute us, it would have been the dullest of sea-side outings. But like a watchful cook stirring the jam, Eoin was introducing them all to each other the whole time. He could glamorize even the dullest. This one's aunt had swum the Channel, that one's brother had been in the San Francisco earthquake or as a girl she had known Fanny Parnell. Sometimes a stray sentence expanded into an immense anecdote, breeding other anecdotes, startling and complex but never malicious. If one of them were to end sadly like 'then the poor fellow took to drink and fell down a lift shaft in Las Vegas', it was like a wreath laid on a tomb. To be remembered by Eoin was to be honoured.

HUBERT BUTLER, *Escape from the Anthill*

NINA

The sunken bath had been made for Nina Kirkwood, an old maiden aunt of the Major's, who was almost paralysed by arthritis for many years and could not have climbed into a bath above the floor. The shape into which the rigid joints of her legs and hips had set was peculiar to her, for never since childhood had she walked more than four steps outside a house, three to a mounting block and one up on to it, or three to the groom who stood by the door and gave her a leg up on to her horse. She rode everywhere, even to the gate lodge or across the one field to the Maxwells' house only five minutes' walk from the stableyard; and of course she always rode side-saddle and rode all day except for church and meal-times, enjoying most of her social life and conversation in the open air with friends who sat on horses more often than chairs. So it happened that after arthritis began during her middle age, her legs became gradually immovable from the position they were accustomed to and when not on a horse she had at last to be held up or carried, because she was like a crane in shallow water with one leg curled and the other straight. Her right leg raised, as though to tuck itself about the pummel, was lost and unsteady without the comfort of pressure below the knee. When her straight leg rested on the ground she longed for the give and movement of a stirrup. She looked like any other woman when she was in the saddle and more graceful than most.

DAVID THOMSON, Woodbrook

THE POET AND HIS WIFE

The poet had a great character when he was young. It's often I heard my mother talking of him. She was alive in his day. He had great stuff and spirit in him – he'd leap every dyke as he went to Mass of a Sunday; and he was always to be remarked among the men near him for his carriage and his character. I knew his character better than anybody else though he was old in my day. I fancy that his first nest – that is to say, his cradle – was in Ballinaráha in Dunquin. He married into the Island, a woman of the Manning family, a marvellous woman. She it was who finished the bailiffs and the drivers who used to come here day after day ruining the poor, who had nothing to live on but famine. A bailiff climbed on to the roof of her house and started knocking it down on her and on to her flock of feeble children. She seized a pair of new shears and opened them – one point this way, the other that. A stout woman and a mad woman! The bailiff never noticed anything till he felt the point of the shears stuck right into his behind. It wasn't the roof of the house that came in through

the hole this time, but a spurt of his blood. That's the last
bailiff we've seen.

TOMAS O'CROHAN, *The Island Man* (Trans. Robin
Flower)

HUMOUR

The Irish do not *make* jokes, in the manner of the Scots (Shaw
– the tireless and unabashed Candid Friend – is to my sense
far more Scot than Irishman); they do not recognise a joke to
which they are not accustomed; they often do not know that
what they are saying is amusing. They simply talk a humorous
language. Almost every drollery one hears in Ireland will be
found to be (in the Gaelic phrase) 'as old as the mist'. It is life
and love and the flesh – and not any mere trifles – that to the
Irishman are ridiculous.

When the English say the Irish have 'lost their sense of
humour' they are thinking of the 'rollicking' Irishman, a
character they could like and understand. They liked him for
the good reason that he was in fact an Englishman – a colonial
variety of the jolly English squire.

MAD OR MALEVOLENT?

An Irishman usually has to be drunk or under anaesthetics
before you can catch him without his slightly mocking inscru-
tability. One may put the matter cruelly and say the Irishman
is always afraid – afraid of his thoughts, his desires, his neighbours. Or one may put it kindly and say that his pride or his
fastidiousness are forever holding him back – that he remains
disdainfully ironical before sensual passion or communal purpose. At his best he is like some mad king of legend, in a world
of tamed, groomed citizens; at his worst he suggests some
rather malevolent gnome from the roots of the hills.

ARLAND USSHER, *The Face and Mind of Ireland*

'Do you like my garden?'

'No,' he said clearly, 'it is very dull.' Quite taken aback, I exclaimed, 'What do you mean?'

'I mean that it is very dull. Don't you think so?'

'Don't you think my initials are well done?'

'Yes, but I don't care for them done in bedding plants, even if they are your initials.'

'The gardener wanted to do the family crest, but as it's a pig, I wouldn't let him,' I told him.

'Oh, you should have; it would have been the perfect culmination of absurdity,' he replied.

Oscar got quite excited picturing how the picture could be done, suggesting flesh-coloured begonias for the body and a houseleek, round and prickly for the eye, and love-lies-bleeding pegged down in twiddles for the tail.

Lady Ardilaun's account of a visit to her by Oscar Wilde,
aged eighteen

INTERVIEW WITH A CLERIC IN KILKENNY

These people have all the divine virtues. They have the faith. No one is a better Christian than the Irishman. Their morals are pure. Their crimes are very rarely premeditated. But they lack essentially the civil virtues. They are without foresight, without prudence. Their courage is instinctive. They throw themselves at an obstacle with extraordinary violence and if they are not successful at the first attempt, they tire of it. They are changeable, love excitement, combat. The Englishman, on the contrary, coldly calculates the odds, approaches danger slowly, and withdraws only after having succeeded.

ALEXIS DE LA TOCQUEVILLE, Journey in Ireland

AN EYE FOR REALITY

The first generalization, then, that can be risked about the Irish character is that the tension between dream and reality is fundamental to it. The fact that the Irish claim to be realists

confirms the view: no one has so cold and startled an eye for
reality as the man who suddenly wakes up.

V. S. PRITCHETT, *At Home and Abroad*

FROM 'AUTUMN JOURNAL'

Why do we like being Irish? Partly because
  It gives us a hold on the sentimental English
As members of a world that never was,
  Baptized with fairy water;

. . .

  Let the games be played in Gaelic.
Let them grow beet-sugar; let them build
  A factory in every hamlet;
Let them pigeon-hole the souls of the killed
  Into sheep and goats, patriots and traitors.
And the North, where I was a boy,
  Is still the North, veneered with the grime of
    Glasgow,
Thousands of men whom nobody will employ
  Standing at the corners, coughing.
And the street-children play on the wet
  Pavement – hopscotch or marbles;
And each rich family boasts a sagging tennis-net
  On a spongy lawn beside a dripping shrubbery.
The smoking chimneys hint
  At prosperity round the corner
But they make their Ulster linen from foreign lint
  And the money that comes in goes out to make
    more money.

. . .

Send her no more fantasy, no more longings which
  Are under a fatal tariff.
For common sense is the vogue
  And she gives her children neither sense nor
    money
Who slouch around the world with a gesture and a
    brogue
  And a faggot of useless memories.

LOUIS MACNEICE, *Collected Poems*

THREE THINGS

It was not for hatred or love of any tribe beyond another, nor at the order of anyone, nor in hope to get gain out of it, that I took in hand to write the history of Ireland, but because I thought it was not fitting that a country like Ireland for honour, and races as honourable as every race that inhabited it, should be swallowed up without any word or mention to be left about them.

If it happens, indeed, that the land is praised by every historian who has written about Ireland, the people are dispraised by every new foreign historian who has written about them, and the thing that stirred me up to write this history of the Irish is the greatness of the pity I felt at the plain injustice that is done to them by these writers. If only, indeed, they had given their true report about the Irish, I do not know why they should not have been put in comparison with any race in Europe, in three things, as they are in bravery, in learning, and in being steadfast to the Catholic faith . . .

GEOFFREY KEATING (Trans. J. M. Synge in *Prose Works*)

HAIL AND FAREWELL

OPEN HOUSE

The hospitality of Dublin is almost embarrassing to an English visitor. If a stranger knows one person he soon knows hundreds. They open their houses to him and let him find his way about. There can be no other capital in the world more generous in its welcome and more devastating in its disapproval. For through Irish life and conversation there runs a bitter spitefulness that at first puzzles you until you understand that it is a national gift. A Catholic bishop once told Padraic Colum that spite and envy are the Catholic vices – the other side of the Catholic virtue of equality – just as harsh individualism and snobbery are the Protestant vices. There may be something in this, in spite of the fact that these vices seem to me shared in equal parts by Catholics and Protestants! But it is a fact that the Irish have a genius for satire. When they get together they love to tell stories that reveal those whom they admire, or those who are important and prominent, in a rather cruelly amusing and belittling light. It is rather confusing at first.

A stranger lost in the confusing maze of Irish conversation feels at first that nothing is sacred to these people until, finding himself outside in the small hours in company with a man who has been sparkling all evening, he discovers that the former brilliance of his companion has been thrown off as an actor throws off a cloak after a play. The amusing Touchstone of the evening becomes a sombre Hamlet. As he walks through the empty street he contradicts everything he has previously said in a voice that comes out from him drenched in an abysmal melancholy.

You then realize that talk in Ireland is a game with no rules.

H. V. MORTON, *In Search of Ireland*

ATLANTIC AIR

The Irish air is Atlantic air, but quite unlike, for instance, that of Maine; it is air empowered by the west wind, moist and rain-smelling, the lethargic air of heathery islands that are surrounded even more by air than by sea. One is excited and half asleep by turns.

In certain weathers, especially in the west of Ireland, where the clouds seem to have been just that minute born out of the sea and to drift about not knowing where to go, Ireland itself almost seems to be newborn. A child could have dabbled it out in simple colours from a paint box. It is more than an emerald isle – it is an ephemeral one. This is, we know, a trick of the Atlantic climate and its light, for there will be hours when the trick is not played – long, gray, heavy hours when the island looks sullen and *is* sullen. No other island is so moody and variable in aspect, so likely to pass from the earthly to the unearthly before our eyes.

V. S. PRITCHETT, *At Home and Abroad*

IRELAND WITH EMILY

Bells are booming down the bohreens,
  White the mist along the grass.
Now the Julias, Maeves and Maureens
  Move between the fields to Mass.
Twisted trees of small green apple
Guard the decent whitewashed chapel,
Gilded gates and doorway grained
Pointed windows richly stained
  With many-coloured Munich glass.

See the black-shawled congregations
  On the broidered vestment gaze
Murmur past the painted stations
  As Thy Sacred Heart displays
Lush Kildare of scented meadows,
Roscommon, thin in ash-tree shadows,
And Westmeath the lake-reflected,
Spreading Leix the hill-protected,
  Kneeling all in silver haze?

In yews and woodbine, walls and guelder,
  Nettle-deep the faithful rest,
Winding leagues of flowering elder,

102

Sycamore with ivy dressed,
Ruins in demesnes deserted,
Bog-surrounded bramble-skirted –
Townlands rich or townlands mean as
These, oh, counties of them screen us
    In the Kingdom of the West.

Stony seaboard, far and foreign,
    Stony hills poured over space,
Stony outcrop of the Burren,
    Stones in every fertile place,
Little fields with boulders dotted,
Grey-stone shoulders saffron-spotted,
Stone-walled cabins thatched with reeds,
Where a Stone Age people breeds
    The last of Europe's stone age race.

Has it held, the warm June weather?
    Draining shallow sea-pools dry,
When we bicycled together
    Down the bohreens fuchsia-high
Till there rose, abrupt and lonely,
A ruined abbey, chancel only,
Lichen-crusted, time-befriended,
Soared the arches, splayed and splendid,
    Romanesque against the sky.

There in pinnacled protection,
    One extinguished family waits
A Church of Ireland resurrection
    By the broken, rusty gates.
Sheepswool, straw and droppings cover,
Graves of spinster, rake and lover,
Whose fantastic mausoleum
Sings its own seablown Te Deum,
    In and out the slipping slates.

JOHN BETJEMAN, *Collected Poems*

Labour Day [1 May] 1952 Up the   White's
Workers of the World down with
la vie de château

Darling Nancy,

Among the countless blessings I thank God for, my failure
to find a house in Ireland comes first. Unless one is mad or
fox hunting there is nothing to draw one. The houses, except
for half-a-dozen famous ones, are very shoddy in building and
they none of them have servants' bedrooms because at the
time they were built Irish servants slept on the kitchen floor.
The peasants are malevolent. All their smiles are false as Hell.
Their priests are very suitable for them but not for foreigners.
No coal at all. Awful incompetence everywhere. No native
capable of doing the simplest job properly.

> From Evelyn Waugh to Nancy Mitford,
> *Evelyn Waugh's Letters* ed. Mark Amory

REMINDERS OF HOME

We had with us in our open coach two young men, each being
very drunk. These young men aimed words at and made jokes
to nearly all the passers-by. All, men and women, responded
with laughter and other jokes. I thought I was in France.

> ALEXIS DE LA TOCQUEVILLE, *Journey in Ireland*

A GREAT STONE BOX

We [Virginia and Leonard] have had a most garrulous time.
We never stop talking. The Irish are the most gifted people in
that line. After dinner the innkeeper comes in and sits down
and talks till bedtime, perfect English, much more amusing
than any London society . . . We spent a night with the Bow-
ens, where, to our horror we found the Connollys – a less
appetising pair I have never seen out of the Zoo, and the
apes are considerably preferable to Cyril. She has the face of
a golliwog and they brought the reek of Chelsea with them
. . . Elizabeth's home was merely a great stone box, but full of

Italian mantelpieces and decayed eighteenth-century furniture, and carpets all in holes – however they insisted on keeping up a ramshackle kind of state, dressing for dinner and so on.

From Virginia Woolf to Vanessa Bell, May 1934,
Letters, v. 5, The Sickle Side of the Moon

On the 15th September 1841, I landed in Dublin, without an acquaintance in the country, and with only two or three letters of introduction from a brother clerk in the Post Office. I had learned to think that Ireland was a land flowing with fun and whiskey, in which irregularity was the rule of life, and where broken heads were looked upon as honourable badges. I was to live at a place called Banagher, on the Shannon, which I had heard of because of its having once been conquered, though it had heretofore conquered everything, including the devil. And from Banagher my inspecting tours were to be made, chiefly into Connaught, but also over a strip of country eastwards, which would enable me occasionally to run up to Dublin. I went to a hotel which was very dirty, and after dinner I ordered some whiskey punch. There was an excitement in this, but when the punch was gone I was very dull. It seemed so strange to be in a country in which there was not a single individual whom I had ever spoken to or ever seen.

ANTHONY TROLLOPE, *Autobiography*

THE NATURE, CUSTOMS AND CHARACTERISTICS OF THE PEOPLE

I have thought it not superfluous to say a few things about the nature of this people both in mind and body, that is to say, of their mental and physical characteristics.

To begin with: when they are born, they are not carefully nursed as is usual. For apart from the nourishment with which they are sustained by their hard parents from dying altogether, they are for the most part abandoned to nature. They are not put in cradles, or swathed; nor are their tender limbs helped by frequent baths or formed by any useful art. The midwives do not use hot water to raise the nose, or press down the face, or lengthen the legs. Unaided nature according to her own judgement arranges and disposes without the help of any art the limbs that she has produced.

As if to prove what she can do by herself she continually shapes and moulds, until she finally forms and finishes them in their full strength with beautiful upright bodies and handsome and well-complexioned faces.

But although they are fully endowed with natural gifts, their external characteristics of beard and dress, and internal cultivation of the mind, are so barbarous that they cannot be said to have any culture . . .

They do not devote their lives to the processing of flax or wool, or to any kind of merchandise or mechanical art. For given only to leisure, and devoted only to laziness, they think that the greatest pleasure is not to work, and the greatest wealth is to enjoy liberty.

This people is, then, a barbarous people, literally barbarous. Judged according to modern ideas, they are uncultivated, not only in the external appearance of their dress, but also in their flowing hair and beards. All their habits are the habits of barbarians. Since conventions are formed from living together in society, and since they are so removed in these distant parts from the ordinary world of men, as if they were in another world altogether and consequently cut off from well-behaved and law-abiding people, they know only of the barbarous habits in which they were born and brought up, and embrace them as another nature. Their natural qualities are excellent. But almost everything acquired is deplorable.

GIRALDUS CAMBRENSIS, *History and Topography of Ireland* (Trans. John O'Meara)

LUGGALA

We had met our fellow-guests in Dublin and driven to Luggala with them. Incredible beauty lay before us as we climbed the last ridge before dipping into the valley – range upon range of mountains spread around us with their tops still golden in the setting sun, and the deep, green, lost valley below. A big loch of brown peaty water with sheep browsing round a small formal temple, and beneath the domed forehead of a crag the house itself – a fantastically pretty white building in purest Strawberry Hill Gothic style. The front door was opened and we were at once in the hall-dining-room, where a huge fire blazed and an oval table laid for dinner filled nearly all the space. What a magical atmosphere that house had, charmingly furnished and decorated to match its style, dim lights, soft music playing and Irish voices ministering seductively to our needs. In the drawing-room stood Oonagh with her hair down her back, and in her short diaphanous dress looking exactly like the fairy off a Christmas tree.

Ralph and I were borne off to our little bedroom where yet another roaring fire was being lit and our things unpacked. The prettiness of the room itself, the humble bathroom next door where the softest dark brown water smelling of peat awaited us, all made up a work of art whoever was responsible, and a contrast to many of the houses of the rich where one may find a single match sticking out of its box as if one were too weak to take it oneself, and inadequate heating. We were led through another room where Tara, Oonagh's youngest boy, was ensconced in the bath. Gareth aged thirteen, with a husky breaking voice and a passion for wild flowers, had appeared during dinner with some friends carrying autograph books in which we were all told to draw or write something *very* funny. When we climbed into bed I for one felt soaked through and through in this pleasant Irish atmosphere.

FRANCES PARTRIDGE, *Everything to Lose*

THE OTHER ISLAND

The plain of Tipperary is the richest farm land in Western Europe, so fertile that farming there requires little skill; beasts are simply left in the fields until they are fat enough to be sold. It is beautiful beyond words and empty. People leave Eire as they have always left Ireland, at an enormous rate. Every village, however small and poor, has a luggage shop. The plan on which the villages are built, one long, immensely wide street which can be used as a market, bordered by tiny houses, accentuates their emptiness. The admirable roads are bare of traffic – for miles and miles there is nothing except, occasionally, an enormous man spanking along in a donkey cart or a Rolls-Royce with American tourists buried in white satin luggage. The cottagers' dogs are so unused to motor traffic that they crouch and spring dangerously at passing cars. The green deserted fields lying beneath blue deserted mountains; the windowless mills dripping with creepers; the towers for captive princesses inhabited by owl and raven; the endless walls surrounding ghostly demesnes, the lodge gates, rusted up and leading into hay; the roofless churches, with elegant neo-Gothic spires rising out of nettle-beds make a melancholy but enchanted impression.

. . .

The village is a splendid shopping centre. It has not yet got a boutique (pronounced bowtike), like Clonmel, but the draper, whose white china horse in the window proclaims him to be a Protestant, has a range of lovely cotton dresses for 12s. 6d., and I stock up with his nylons for the whole year. Medical Hall keeps French cosmetics and scent. Next door to where it says 'Yoke your Team to a Pierce Machine' there is an exciting new notice: Modern Hairstyling. I ask about it in Medical Hall. Oh yes, there are two young ladies trained in New York and they wash your hair backwards. The young ladies have already lost some of the transatlantic hustle, I note. It is half past eleven when I ring their bell; the receptionist is still in her dressing-gown. However, my hair is beautifully washed and the bill is 6s.

NANCY MITFORD, A Talent to Annoy

THE BLUE EYE
(after St Colm Cille)

There's a sea-blue eye that stares
At Ireland drawing away.

It will never look again
At the women of Ireland, or its men.

SEAN DUNNE, *The Sheltered Nest*

FROM 'VALEDICTION'

Therefore I resign, good-bye the chequered and the
    quiet hills
The gaudily-striped Atlantic, the linen-mills
That swallow the shawled file, the black moor where
    half
A turf-stack stands like a ruined cenotaph;
Good-bye your hens running in and out of the white
    house
Your absent-minded goats along the road, your black
    cows
Your greyhounds and your hunters beautifully bred
Your drums and your dolled-up Virgins and your
    ignorant dead.

LOUIS MACNEICE, *Collected Poems*

EMIGRATION

We stood, in the month of June, on the Quay of Cork to see
some emigrants embark in one of the steamers for Falmouth,
on their way to Australia. The band of exiles amounted to two
hundred, and an immense crowd had assembled to bid them
a long and last adieu. The scene was touching to a degree;
it was impossible to witness it without heart-pain and tears.
Mothers hung upon the necks of their athletic sons; young
girls clung to elder sisters; fathers – old white-headed men –
fell upon their knees, with arms uplifted to heaven, imploring

the protecting care of the Almighty on their departing children. 'Och,' exclaimed one aged woman, 'all's gone from me in the wide world when you're gone! Sure you was all I had left! – of seven sons – but you! Oh Dennis, Dennis, never forget your mother – your mother! – don't, avourneen – your poor ould mother, Dennis!' and Dennis, a young man – though the sun was shining on his grey hair – supported 'his mother' in his arms until she fainted, and then he lifted her into a small car that had conveyed his baggage to the vessel, and kissing a weeping young woman who leaned against the horse, he said, 'I'll send home for you both, Peggy, in the rise of next year; and ye'll be a child to her from this out, till then, and *then* avourneen you'll be my own.' When we looked again the young man was gone, and 'Peggy' had wound her arms round the old woman, while another girl held a broken cup of water to her lips. Amid the din, the noise, the turmoil, the people pressing and rolling in vast masses towards the place of embarkation like the waves of the troubled sea, there were many such sad episodes.

MR AND MRS HALL, *Ireland: Scenery and Character*
1825–40

A REAL IRISH GRIEVANCE

The Irish possess a happy power of adaptation to the habits and customs of the people they sojourn among. In Ireland, the Macnamaras held the position of County magnates, living in a grand old Mansion with extensive demesne – hunting the County with their own pack – and exercising hospitality on such a lavish scale as to render Absenteeism an absolute necessity. Yet, upon their removal to Cheltenham, where they occupied a hired house in a Square, jobbed carriage and horses for the Season, and kept one hack for the Son, they took to their new life as complacently and readily as if they had never moved in any other sphere.

My Aunt was congratulating Mr and Mrs Macnamara upon exchanging the life at Ballyshan Castle, which was miserably dull and violently rollicking by turns, with the uniformly cheerful and sociable life at Cheltenham.

'You do not seem to take into account,' smiled Mr Macnamara, 'the loss of dignity which that change has brought us. We are no longer among the heads of a great County, but are mingled up among undistinguished gentry. Would you like to come down from your grandeur as the lady of Canon Haughton and become plain, simple Mrs Haughton?'

My Aunt, not perceiving that Mr Macnamara was speaking ironically, exclaimed energetically, 'That I would; and I heartily wish I could prevail upon the Canon to follow your example in making England his home. There is one objection he could not get over – the English look down on the Irish, and seldom miss an opportunity of claiming superiority over them. At least I have been told that it is so; you have been here long enough to know whether it is true.'

'Never in society,' replied Mr Macnamara, 'unless when provoked by some of our pretentious bragging countrymen. And even then it is done in a quiet, though effective way. As when, for instance, an Irishman boasts of his Country being the finest country in the world, possessing the most charming climate and the grandest scenery, the best hunting, fishing, and shooting; he is met with, "O, indeed, you surprise me; but pray, tell me, if Ireland be such as you describe, how is it that there are so many Absentees?" When, however, it becomes a matter of *business* between an Englishman and an Irishman, then the national characteristic of the former comes out strong; caution in their dealing with us, and distrust of our professions. Old Kendrick, whose daughter is engaged to my son, brings his Solicitor to me, who first inspects my Title-deeds, and then wrings out of me all the charges upon the estate; and, upon my proposing that the girl's money should be handed over to me, and I would charge the Estate with a sum sufficient for the proper maintenance of the young couple until my death, he coolly informs me that the estate has already so many charges upon it that it resembles a target so riddled with bullets that there was hardly space for another bullet mark.'

ANON, *Some Time in Ireland*

111

Lord and Lady Leytrim and Son and Daughter and two or three Irish Cousins came here in a party from Dublin and had fancied themselves excessively fine and Tonish because his Lordship had amassed a great fortune by being employed under Government who had rewarded him for cheating the Public with an Irish Barony which his daughter made use of to take place of every one, whether her right or no, and in short the whole family had given themselves most amazing Airs and in particular had treated Lady Liddell and your humble Servant *de hot and Bass* on our first arrival. Now it so happens that *undeservedly* I am now looked up to as the very first Ton of Spa and no Party is arranged without first consulting my Ladyship, and not one of them can these unhappy Irish get into but are left out as Rubbish, and now they are as mean and fawning as they were before insolent, but it is too late and they have no chance of recovering the least degree of importance . . .

From the Hon. Judith Milbanke to Mary Noel, 1786,
The Noels and the Milbankes

FINEST IN THE WORLD

Where are our missing twenty millions of Irish should be here today instead of four, our lost tribes? And our potteries and textiles, the finest in the whole world! And our wool that was sold in Rome in the time of Juvenal and our flax and our damask from the looms of Antrim and our Limerick lace, our tanneries and our white flint glass down there by Ballybough and our Huguenot poplin that we have since Jacquard de Lyon and our woven silk and our Foxford tweeds and ivory raised point from the Carmelite convent in New Ross, nothing like it in the whole wide world! Where are the Greek merchants that came through the pillars of Hercules, the Gibraltar now grabbed by the foe of mankind, with gold and Tyrian purple to sell in Wexford at the fair of Carmen? Read Tacitus and Ptolemy, even Giraldus Cambrensis. Wine, peltries, Connemara marble, silver from Tipperary, second to none, our far-famed horses even today, the Irish hobbies, with king Philip of Spain offering to pay customs duties for the right to fish in our waters. What do the yellow-johns of Anglia owe us for our ruined trade and our ruined hearths?

JAMES JOYCE, Ulysses

THE VILLAGE OF LONGING

The gaudy clothes, the speech dented by Cockney, the boastful street-corner bombast about drink and women (mostly, and more feelingly, about drink), seem now merely flesh wounds in the war of nerves in which every emigrant serves. Style and manner – some people even came home with new walks, rapid city struts; not always confined to girls in impossible (and surely sinful!) stiletto heels, either – were understandable blemishes, predictable deformities, tolerable insignia of altered lives.

Of course, they were 'shoving on', 'shaping', 'trying to cut a dash'. Why not? Even then, as I took in the criticism, I didn't see what fuelled it. I found myself more naturally drawn to the know-nothing exuberance of the temporarily returned, their longing to make a splash, their cultural anarchy. And this was only partly because I detested the asperity of our kitchen council, not for its lack of charity, since I had no moral self-consciousness then, but because its atmosphere made me feel intimidated, fearful, frail.

Besides, why shouldn't they have their holiday, their hulla-baloo? Why shouldn't they feel cocky, now that they'd paid off the family debt to the town's hucksters? Everyone could eat sweet-cake now for a fortnight and real rashers too, not the customary handful of scraps from the bacon-slicer. Gin-and-limes could be consumed too, by the bucketful if needs be, though all the stay-at-home world would dispute its claim to be a proper drink. And, long after midnight, let the street resound to the cracked tenors and 'Hear my song, Violetta!'

If there was a deliberate undertow of *épater* to such carous-ing, so much the better, I thought. Because in one respect I knew Mam's criticisms to be true (Mam, source and inspiration of Swiss Cottage class-consciousness): these show-off visitors were nobodies. As soon as they turned Parks Road corner, making for the station with their flat, cardboard suitcases, they effectively resumed their anonymous lives: their hand-callousing, noisy, repetitive lives; their dirty, lonesome, well-paid lives. So weren't they right to act like somebodies when they could?

GEORGE O'BRIEN, The Village of Longing

AFTER A CHILDHOOD AWAY FROM IRELAND

One summer
we slipped in at dawn,
on plum-coloured water
in the sloppy quiet.

The engines
of the ship stopped.
There was an eerie
drawing-near,

a noiseless coming head-on
of red roofs, walls,
dogs, barley stooks.
Then we were there.

Cobh.
Coming home.
I had heard of this:
the ground the emigrants

resistless, weeping,
laid their cheeks to,
put their lips to kiss.
Love is also memory.

I only stared.
What I had lost
was not land
but the habit of land:

whether of growing out of,
or settling back on,
or being
defined by.

I climb
to your nursery.
I stand listening
to the dissonances

of the summer's day ending.
I bend to kiss you.
Your cheeks
are brick pink.

EAVAN BOLAND, Outside History

Out of such stuff as Ireland dreams are made. . . . I haven't
thought of Ireland for ten years, and tonight in an hour's space
I have dreamed Ireland from end to end. When shall I think
of her again? In another ten years; that will be time enough
to think of her again. And on these words I climbed the long
stone stairs leading to my garret.

One of Ireland's many tricks is to fade away to a little speck
down on the horizon of our lives, and then to return suddenly
in tremendous bulk, frightening us. My words were: In
another ten years it will be time enough to think of Ireland
again. But Ireland rarely stays away so long.

GEORGE MOORE, Hail and Farewell

GUESTING AND FEASTING

As an expression of welcome, a person says, 'We'll spread green rushes under your feet.'

P. W. JOYCE, *English As We Speak It In Ireland*

A COUNTRY QUADRILLE

I swallowed a pint of rascally sherry without a murmur, fortified it with a dose of diluted alcohol, yawned my way to my room, found clean linen – no fire, and, in five minutes, was buried in sleep 'fast as a watchman'.

Presently arose a hum of many voices; dreams and phantasies disturbed my uneasy slumbers; a noise like distant music at times was faintly audible; at last a crash of instruments awoke me, and the first quadrille was in full execution within four feet of my distracted head!

Heaven granted me patience, although I was on the very brink of a country ball-room, and separated from 'the gay throng' only by the intervention of a slip of deal board, while through the chinks you might have passed the poker, or interchanged a parasol.

I raised myself up on my elbow, and what a group was there! A short man, in a claret-coloured coat, was paired with a stout gentlewoman in bright scarlet: she must have been descended from 'the giant'; I would as soon grapple with her in a waltz as commit myself to the embraces of a boa-constrictor. *Vis-à-vis* was a police-officer, in state uniform, with a pale beauty in cerulean blue; and a personage of immense calf, in black *tights*, confronted a skeleton in nankeen *unmentionables*. The ladies were gloriously adorned with silver ribbon, gilt wreaths, and every flower that blows, from a pink to a peony; the lords of the creation sported stiffened cravats and a plurality of waistcoats; and the ball-room emitted 'an ancient and fish-like smell' – a miasm of musk, assisted by every abomination in perfumery.

I was in an intermediate state between frenzy and fever, and turned over in my mind the expediency of setting fire to the bed-curtains, and sending myself, the quadrille, and the whole company to the skies, by igniting ten pounds of Harvey's *treble strong*, which was stowed away somewhere in my luggage. Did tired nature quiesce for a moment, I was fearfully roused with a tornado of torturous sounds. 'Places, gentlemen!' – 'Ladies' chain!' – 'Now, don't dance, Patsey; you know you're drunk!' – 'Arrah! Charley, are you stupid?' – *'Dos-à-dos, Miss Rourke!'* – 'Up with the Lancers!' – 'Aisy, Mr Bodkin! remember there are ladies here!' – 'Waiter! there's porter wanted at the card-table!' Somnus! deity of my adoration! never expose me to such misery as I endured in the archiepiscopal town of Tuam!

Morning came, and the company retired to supper below stairs. Anticipating the consequences, I fortified my chamber-door with all the moveables I could collect. It was a prudent precaution; for, blessed be God! a row ensued, that finished both delph and dancing. I suffered nothing in person, but my less-fortunate valet got a black eye from a Connemara gentleman, who, unluckily for poor Travers, mistook him for the master of the ceremonies, with whom he of Connemara was at feud.

W. H. MAXWELL, *Wild Sports of the West*

ANCESTRAL DANCE

In the bar the evening had begun. A young man was playing an accordion and across the room people were lined along the bench under the window with tables before them.

Couples turned sedately in waltz time. A woman in a shining green dress, another in a pair of black slacks danced with men in white shirts and ties and coats fitting tight across the shoulders. One wondered at the number of dancers for there seemed so few women in the room. Except for two women near the door only men lined the bench under the window; old men and young men wearing caps and jackets, their black shoes showing under the tables in a corresponding line. Beneath the caps raw faces received a steady glass; black Guinness stout stood on all the tables.

A large family, every one of them in spectacles, surrounded a table near us. One of the bespectacled children helped the barmaid service the tables.

The accordion began a reel and the dancers formed two

lines. They turned in place, one hand on hip, the other in the air, the fingers gracefully held aloft; the toes point to the side, then cross the ankle in a diminutive entre-chat.

Here is the ancestral dance of the ballet, refined by the brilliant galliards and stately pavanes of the court. The movement is in the legs, the torso and arms taking static positions in accompaniment.

The dancers were very good, though the shiny binding dress ill-graced the slow hops and lifting arms, and the slacks hid the most beautiful aspect of the body in these dances. Even an ungainly leg rearranged by the pointing toe becomes graceful.

Some of the men wore the Pioneer's pin in their lapels, a shield bearing a red cross and a heart that signifies voluntary abstention from alcohol. Yet the atmosphere got closer, the drinking more telling – a mood of sad abandon seemed to overtake the room. A voice called from outside the crowded door, and everyone stopped and looked as a man left his partner on the floor and hurried to the door. The faces watching looked sympathetic but unworried. Perhaps there was a wife outside who had come before, on other Fridays.

The accordion player sang, his head thrown back, lost in the music and his own yearnings. The words cried out, 'Return to the wild side of life.' P said, 'It's the same tune as our "I've Got Pins and Needles in My Heart."'

Requests were called out, among them 'Danny Boy'. Like those of drunken Irishmen, the tears gushed from their secret source and rolled down my face. The music, all by itself, came from and calls to that place where dwells the helpless sense of splendour in all Life and the unreconciled pain of its end.

DEBORAH LOVE, *Annagh Keen*

FRESH TROUT

Having caught enough trout to satisfy any moderate appetite, like true sportsmen the gentlemen on board our boat became eager to hook a salmon. Had they hooked a few salmons, no doubt they would have trolled for whales, or for a mermaid; one of which finny beauties the waterman swore he had seen on the shore of Derryclear, he with Jim Mullen being above on a rock, the mermaid on the shore directly beneath them, visible to the middle, and as usual 'racking her hair.' It was fair hair, the boatman said; and he appeared as convinced of the existence of the mermaid, as he was of the trout just landed in the boat.

The attempts on the salmon having failed, the rain continuing to fall steadily, the Herd's cottage before named was resorted to: when Marcus, the boatman, commenced forthwith to gut the fish, and, taking down some charred turf-ashes from the blazing fire, on which about a hundredweight of potatoes were boiling, he – Marcus – proceeded to grill on the floor some of the trout, which we afterwards ate with immeasurable satisfaction. They were such trouts as, when once tasted, remain for ever in the recollection of a commonly grateful mind – rich, flaky, creamy, full of flavour. A Parisian *gourmand* would have paid ten francs for the smallest *cooleen* among them; and, when transported to his capital, how different in flavour would they have been! – how inferior to what they were as we devoured them, fresh from the fresh waters of the lake, and jerked as it were from the water to the gridiron! The world had not had time to spoil those innocent beings before they were gobbled up with pepper and salt, and missed, no doubt, by their friends. I should like to know more their '*set*'. But enough of this: my feelings overpower me: suffice it to say, they were red or salmon trouts – none of your white-fleshed brown-skinned river fellows.

When the gentlemen had finished their repast, the boatmen and the family set to work upon the ton of potatoes, a number of the remaining fish, and a store of other good things; then we all sat round the turf-fire in the dark cottage, the rain coming down steadily outside, and veiling everything except the shrubs and verdure immediately about the cottage. The Herd, the Herd's wife, and a nondescript female friend, two healthy young herdsmen in corduroy rags, the herdsman's daughter paddling about with bare feet, a stout black-eyed wench with her gown over her head, and a red petticoat not quite so good as new, the two boatmen, a badger just killed and turned inside out, the gentlemen, some hens cackling and flapping about among the rafters, a calf in a corner cropping green meat and occasionally visited by the cow her mama, formed the society of the place. It was rather a strange picture; but as for about two hours we sat there, and maintained an almost unbroken silence, and as there was no other amusement but to look at the rain, I began, after the enthusiasm of the first half-hour, to think that after all London was a bearable place, and that for want of a turf-fire and a bench in Connemara, one *might* put up with a sofa and a newspaper in Pall Mall.

WILLIAM THACKERAY, *The Irish Sketch Book*

POTATOES

Potatoes are really important to Irish people. British Queen are the ones we like to eat in summer and Kerr's Pink followed by Golden Wonder in winter. They are very floury and inclined to break in the cooking water. They should never be peeled before cooking. If they still break, the water must be poured off before they are quite cooked and the potatoes finish cooking in their own steam. They are peeled at table and (ideally) eaten with a big lump of golden butter.

There are a great many Irish potato dishes and some confusion about their names. The two we usually serve are Colcannon which is made with cabbage, and Stelk or Champ made with chives or spring onions.

CARRAGEEN MOSS PUDDING

Ballyandreen is a tiny fishing village by a rocky inlet four miles south of Ballymaloe. For generations the inhabitants there have gathered and sold carrageen moss. It is picked from the farthest out rocks at low water during spring tides in June. This means that it is almost always covered by sea water. It is then laid out on the short grass on the clifftop to dry and bleach in the sun. It has the reputation of being a health-giving food. It is a source of agar jelly. It certainly contains iron and minerals. Traditionally, it was fed to calves and made into cough syrups and milk puddings. I have used it all my life. I have thickened milk for babies with it at weaning time. For

123

more sophisticated meals I serve it topped with whipped cream and coffee sauce strongly laced with whiskey.

A product that is hard to measure, however, is hard to market. This is so with carrageen moss. The success of this dish is in using only just enough to get a set – so that you don't taste it in the pudding, as an unenthusiastic friend pointed out!

Carrageen sometimes comes mixed with grass and other sea-weeds; these should be carefully removed before use.

Picking Carrageen

There are two very similar varieties of carrageen moss, *Gigartina stellata* and *Chondrus crispus*. Both are widely distributed.

They are brownish black or dark green and from 7.5−15 cm/ 3−6 in long. They grow abundantly on the rocks at low tide line.

Pick in early summer at low water during spring tides. Bleach in the sun. Wash occasionally in plenty of cold water then lay out to dry again. When quite white and well dried, bring indoors and store in a jute bag. It will keep for one or two years.

Carrageen Moss Pudding

½ cup cleaned, well-dried carrageen (1 semi-closed fistful)
3¾ cups milk
2 tablesp. sugar
1 egg
½ teasp. vanilla essence or vanilla pod

Serves 4−6. Soak the carrageen in tepid water for 10 minutes. Put in a saucepan with milk and a vanilla pod if used. Bring to the boil and simmer very gently for 20 minutes. Pour through a strainer into a mixing bowl. The carrageen will now be swollen and exuding jelly. Rub all this jelly through the strainer and beat it into the milk and with the sugar, egg yolk and vanilla essence, if used. Test for a set in a saucer as one would with gelatine. Whisk the egg white stiffly and fold it in gently. It will rise to make a fluffy top. Serve chilled with a fruit compote, Caramel or Irish Coffee Sauce.

MYRTLE ALLEN, *Ballymaloe Cookbook*

PARSNIPS AND VIOLETS

I asked her if it would not be possible, now and then, to have a parsnip. A parsnip! she cried, as if I had asked for a dish of sucking Jew. I reminded her that the parsnip season was fast drawing to a close and that if, before it finally got there, she could feed me nothing but parsnips I'd be grateful. I like parsnips because they taste like violets and violets because they smell like parsnips. Were there no parsnips on earth violets would leave me cold and if violets did not exist I would care as little for parsnips as I do for turnips, or radishes.

SAMUEL BECKETT, *First Love*

THE HARVEST DANCE

The ballroom was the grain loft, a long low room that stretched the whole width of the yard above the stables and coach-house. Two casement and two beautiful circular windows looked out from it across the yard to the back of the house and kitchen door, and from the windows on the far side you could see the grass of Shanwelliagh among trees and the Hill of Usna beyond. The ballroom was whitewashed inside and out, its window frames and door pale green like all the paintwork of the stable yard. Its floorboards were wide and even, unpolished except by grain and marred at the corners, or where a knot had fallen out, by ragged holes gnawn by rats. The grain that was spread there after threshing, and turned over again and again till it dried, had nearly all been moved by September and put into bins in the storehouse. Before the dance we shovelled what was left into bags and carried it down on our shoulders, but however carefully we swept the floor there were always a few scattered grains on which the dancers skidded. We sprinkled soapflakes on the boards and arranged planks on boxes along the walls for people to sit on, with a few kitchen chairs for the old ones, whose only difficulty and fear was the steep wooden staircase outside – two flights of creaking steps, some of them rotten, that were the only way into the ballroom. The stairs were a terror to Ivy too, because on those warm nights, when the loft was thick with hundreds of people and the smoke of cut flake from dozens of pipes, as many as could would crowd on to the staircase for air, talking and laughing and pushing each other about in fun, and she thought the whole ancient structure would collapse and throw them in a heap on to the cobbles. We laughed at that and Charlie said from year to year that he would get Nolan, the carpenter, to make a new one next year, until one year it really did collapse. No one was much hurt and Jimmy and I built a concrete staircase in its place. It does not look so pleasant, but when I last saw it two years ago it was still firm.

The weather sometimes stopped us from fixing the date ahead. We would decide in the morning to have the dance that night. Tom, who was a good accordionist and leader of the band, would then be out most of the day on his bicycle gathering the players. One of the fiddlers lived at Ballyfarnan, seven miles to the north; and the best man on the squeeze-box, the old type of melodeon, at Croghan, five miles to the south. Drums and tin whistles were nearer. We would stop the Dublin –Sligo bus which passed Woodbrook gates at about two o'clock and tell the driver to spread the word along the Sligo road. The news would pass from farm to farm at dinner time. No private invitations were needed.

For Phoebe, celebrations began with a children's party at about three o'clock. The outhouses and the wooded garden, sheltered from the north by a high but climbable stone wall, its shrubs, long grass and broken greenhouse were perfectly laid out for hide-and-seek. There was tennis, and swimming from the boat on the lake, and an immense tea, with ham, eggs, bread with thick butter and jam, small sticky cakes made by Winnie, and a birthday cake as wide as the wheel of a barrow into which for days beforehand she had put her energy and pride. The bread, both white and brown, was made by Winnie too, also the butter and jam. Only tea and sugar came from the shop. With both spare leaves inserted, the dining-room table extended from the lakeside window almost to the fireplace. Three double blankets were laid on it and covered by two of the largest white linen tablecloths, patterned with a glazed tracery of leaves and smelling of new starch, which like the highly polished silver teapots and hot water jugs showed Winnie's loving skill again, not a crease to be seen in her ironing, not a faded stain of old spilt tea. Aunt Nina's room was noisy with children and their parents, and Ivy, who believed in life after death, in the survival of the spirit of a person in the place where he or she had lived, once said to me that Nina must be pleased to find her room so filled that had been quiet and lonely for many years.

Meanwhile, one of the Maxwell brothers had taken a farm cart in to Carrick-on-Shannon to fetch a barrel or two of porter. Even with Jim, who walked faster than the other cart-horse, the three miles there and three miles back would take him five hours including of course one hour or more for loading. Its purchase and slow noticeable journey home to Woodbrook made another form of invitation to men working in roadside fields, and was also an inevitable invitation to the Civic Guards. I do not know whether the dance itself was illegal. Perhaps the Kirkwoods should have had a licence for one that welcomed many unknown guests.

It aroused the suspicious attention of the parish priest and the superintendent of the Gardaí. The priest, who never came, but fulminated in chapel the next Sunday, which was sometimes the next morning, against all dances and this one in particular, was impossible to coax. But the superintendent who sent two or three of his men could be set at ease next morning by their reports, because Charlie with the help of the Maxwells always invited them to sit in the coach-house where the barrels were concealed. Except for their uniforms, which inhibited them from dancing in the thundering loft above their heads, they were just like any other countrymen and would spend all night talking about hurling and cattle and racing. Once or twice they would walk out, attracted by an argument, and then sit down again. No arrest was ever made that I remember.

The Harvest Dance was a sensuous meeting between men and women, the more to be feared by the Gardai and priest because in Ireland even linking arms was usually done in private. Men and women separated after each dance, the men gathering at one end of the loft and the women ranging themselves on the planks we had placed against the walls. But the closeness of so many bodies, the smells of soap, tobacco, snuff and all the best scents from the chemists of Boyle and Carrick, made everybody warm. To me, and I daresay to many, the smell of the refreshing ground mist rising from the meadows and the lake, and the perpetual rhythmic croaking of the corn-crakes, was romantic and sad.

DAVID THOMSON, Woodbrook

MRS DELANEY'S BREAKFAST PARTY

Delville, 22 June 1750 – My garden is at present in the high glow of beauty, my cherries ripening, roses, jessamine, and pinks in full bloom, and the hay partly spread and partly in cocks, complete the rural scene. We have discovered a new breakfasting place under the shade of nut-trees, impenetrable to the sun's rays in the midst of a grove of elms, where we shall breakfast this morning; I have ordered cherries, straw-berries, and nosegays to be laid on our breakfast table, and have appointed a harper to be here to play to us during our repast, who is to be hid among the trees. Mrs Hamilton is to breakfast with us, and is to be cunningly led to this place *and surprised*.

Mrs Delaney's Letters

THE DEVIL'S COOKS

God sends meat and the devil sends cooks. So, it pleaseth God to send them plenty of milk, but as they behave themselves in the using of it, it is fit for nobody but for themselves, that are of the uncleanly diet, not only in their milk and butter but in many other unsavoury dishes besides.

It is holden [i.e. believed] among the Irish to be a pre-sagement of some misfortune to keep their milking vessels cleanly, and that if they should either scald or wash them, some unlucky misadventure would surely betide them. Upon this conceit, all the vessels that they use about their milk are most filthily kept: and I myself have seen, that vessel which they hold under the cow whilst they are in milking, to be furred half an inch thick with filth, so that Dublin itself is served every market day with such butter as I am sure is much more loathsome than toothsome.

BARNABY RICH, A New Description of Ireland

When I asked in the hotel for 'drisheen' they thought that I was trying to be funny. They treated me to that snobbish amusement which the Ritz would bestow on a man who was honest enough to demand a black pudding or a pound of tripe. However, I was firm, and in dead earnest, so they promised to send out and buy me a length for luncheon.

This drisheen, which looks like a large and poisonous snake, is a native of Cork, although it is imitated with variations in other parts of Ireland. When real Corkers (but Corkonian is, I believe, the accepted word) leave home on business they often take a yard of drisheen with them into less enlightened cities to delight them, and to proclaim an origin of which no Irishman has ever been ashamed. If you see a man in Waterford, Wexford, Galway, Dublin, or Limerick devouring what appears to be a chocolate-coloured python, you can be certain that he comes from Cork.

Now drisheen is a kind of sausage, made, I understand, mainly from sheep's blood and milk. It is the Irish cousin of the Bury pudding. Superior Dubliners pretend that it bites. They make the same wearisome jests about it that men make about Stilton cheese and haggis. But drisheen is above such low comment: one might call it the caviare of Cork.

'I married an English girl twelve years ago, and we were living in London,' said a Cork man to me, 'and when I had a bad attack of influenza friends in Cork sent me a drisheen. It is the first thing all doctors in Cork give when you are seriously ill, because it is the most nourishing and digestible of all foods. Well, my wife had never seen a drisheen, and when she opened the box it stood up and stretched itself. She screamed and dropped it, thinking it was a snake . . .'

They brought me the drisheen boiled on a plate. When cut it looked like a firm chocolate blancmange. In a moment of mistaken enthusiasm they poured melted butter on it, but I felt instinctively that drisheen lovers employ a less sickly garnish. It is a peculiar, subtle dish, pleasant and ladylike.

I believe that I would like it better fried.

H. V. MORTON, *In Search of Ireland*

Country house life resembles the French *vie de château* more than the quick weekend dash of the English. As in France, small unfortified country houses are called Castle. Guests move in for a good long stay, with their dogs, children, embroidery and fishing-rods. There is generally an invalid to be tenderly inquired for. 'She was wandering this afternoon and then went into such a very sound sleep that I sent for the doctor. He hopes that next time the chemist won't muddle up the labels.' A couple is invited from another part of Ireland; they reply by telegram: 'Bother arrive by car Tuesday.' 'If it's such a bother –' says the hostess crossly until she realizes that the word should be both.

The houses are beautiful in their provincial way and have such romantic names as Ann's Grove, Dereen, Newtown Anner. They are full of treasures (with the oddest attributions, like *Madame du Barry by Largilliere*) in a hotch potch of rubbish. The china cabinet will contain Rose Pompadour Sèvres cheek by jowl with A Present from Bexhill; old *Tatlers* in a bookshelf are muddled up with Oudry's *Fables de La Fontaine*. All this is a happy hunting-ground for dishonest dealers. The famous Irish plaster work is often coarse and rather ugly, too much like the plaster in which somebody's leg has recovered from a Swiss accident stuck on the wall. French gardening amateurs, who arrived in a bus, annoyed one of my hostesses by exclaiming: '*Comme c'est charmant, tout ce désordre britannique!*'

NANCY MITFORD, *A Talent to Annoy*

Dinah concentrated on a group perched on mahogany stools at the distant end of the bar. Sealed into a bubble of tobacco smoke they appeared to her as a rosy mirage, the rasp of their laughter spicy on the mild spread of placatory talk. So groups of people gathered all over Ireland, she imagined, in public houses or village streets, across garden walls, their faces angelic, their breasts radiant with friendship. 'I have a theory,' she confided to Figgis. 'The people of this country are full of kindness, but always to strangers. When a relationship is required – landlady, mother, husband, wife, complications and hostilities arise. They do not have the facility for intimacy.'

'You have the theory, we go one better – we have the formula,' Figgis boasted. 'Consider, if you will, the supreme discomfort of your average Irish home, the low-wattage bulbs, the poor drainage and heating, the wisps of shattered lino marooned on rotting floorboards. Now witness the high degree of cosseting on offer in a common or garden gargle parlour. We Irish were never intended to live in domesticity. The entire scene is so arranged that we are encouraged to flee the austerity and rebuke of home for the comfort of strangers and the cordiality of the shebeen.'

CLARE BOYLAN, *Black Baby*

THE BEST INN IN WATERFORD

Dinner is just over; it is assize-week, and the *table-d'hôte* was surrounded for the chief part by English attorneys – the cyouncillors (as the bar are pertinaciously called) dining upstairs in private. Well, on going to the public room, and being about to lay down my hat on the sideboard, I was obliged to pause – out of regard to a fine thick coat of dust, which had been kindly left to gather for some days past, I should think, and which it seemed a shame to misplace. Yonder is a chair basking quietly in the sunshine; some round object has evidently reposed upon it (a hat or plate probably), for you see a clear circle of black horsehair in the middle of the chair, and dust all round it. Not one of those dirty napkins that the four waiters carry would wipe away the grime from the chair, and take to itself a little dust more! The people in the room are shouting out for the waiters, who cry, 'Yes, sir,' peevishly, and don't come; but stand bawling and jangling, and calling each other names, at the sideboard. The dinner is plentiful and nasty – raw ducks, raw peas, on a crumpled tablecloth, over which a waiter has just spirted a pint of obstreperous cider. The windows are open, to give free view of a crowd of old beggar-women, and of a fellow playing a cursed Irish pipe. Presently

131

this delectable apartment fills with choking peat-smoke; and on asking what is the cause of this agreeable addition to the pleasures of the place, you are told that they are lighting a fire in a back-room.

Why should lighting a fire in a back-room fill a whole enormous house with smoke? Why should four waiters stand and *jaw* and gesticulate among themselves, instead of waiting on the guests? Why should ducks be raw, and dust lie quiet in places where a hundred people pass daily?

WILLIAM THACKERAY, *The Irish Sketch Book*

AN EIGHTEENTH-CENTURY TABLE

Table setting and menu for 15 place settings, served at 3 courses with 9 dishes each.

First course
1. Large joint of beef 'tremblante' garnished with small patés
2. Two soups (one partridge with vegetables in clear stock, one meat (lamb) stock)
3. 4 middle sized entrée dishes including pigeon pie, stuffed veal with parsley and cream, casserole with *vin de bourgogne*
4. 2 small entrée dishes including small chickens with eggs and sauce, and rare mutton

Second course
Large plate of Ham and baked tongue for the middle
2 plates of sugar for the end of the table
4 smaller roasts which include turkey, partridge and hare with accompanying side salads
2 salads for the sides of the table
2 plates of oranges and 2 sauces for the corners of the table
3 side dishes to serve with the roast which include Almond cake garnished with *croquantes*
Apple pie garnished with peaches *en sigovie*

Final course
4 medium dishes for the corners and 2 small dishes for the side

Mushrooms in cream
Foyes gras en ragout
Artichokes with parmesan

Mrs Delaney's Letters

A WALK TO CURRAGHMORE

I returned to the town by the river, the banks of which are well cultivated and very romantic, and I started to walk to Curraghmore, where I arrived tired and breathless about four o'clock. I sent in my letter to the Marquis of Waterford, and, having been received by him very civilly, I asked permission after a few minutes' conversation to retire in order to dress. It was then explained to me that, while dinner would be willingly given, it would not be possible to give me a bed. That embarrassed me a little, as I had not the slightest notion where I could pass the night, but in the end I left the matter to the care of Providence, as is my usual custom.

The Marquis made me sit near him and treated me with singular politeness. He offered me his carriage, in order to conduct me to the inn; his house, he said, was full; he was very sorry, &c. &c. I thanked him for his offer, but declined it, and he then ordered a man to go with me and carry my parcel, which contained nothing other than the clothes which I carry with me. His son even offered me, in parting, another commodity which I absolutely refused, saying that I should be very sorry indeed to be a charge to the friends of the late Mr Burton Conyngham. After having plunged through the mud in pumps and white silk stockings for two or three miles, I arrived at the inn at about half-past ten o'clock. I knocked and asked for a bed, and was told, rudely, by an ugly-looking domestic that I could not have one. I snatched my package from the hands of my lord's servant, saying to report to his master that I had been refused a bed at his inn, and I started off at once at high speed. At the name of the Marquis everybody seemed to be turned upside down. They ran after me, begging me to return.

'I would rather pass the night in Hell,' I said, and promptly consigned them to the inhabitants of that place.

Behind a sheltered wall I put on my travelling clothes, with the intention of walking to Waterford, although it was already eleven o'clock at night. This stoppage gave me time to reflect, and to find that I was already fatigued. I thought it well, in the end, to return to the village and try to get lodging in some other house than the inn. On the way I met the priest of the parish, and explained to him my unfortunate position. My foreign accent determined him, charitably, to leave me to my own devices. This village resembles that to which, according to the fable, Jupiter and Mercury came seeking hospitality and finding their request refused at every door. Like them, in the end, I had to leave the village, and I perceived on the road, in the corner of a ditch, a miserable cabin, the horrible shelter of abjectest poverty. I knocked, and an old woman, another Baucis, clothed in rags, opened the door. I told her that I was a poor traveller who had lost his way, and was tired. She immediately asked me to come in and offered me all that her house afforded – a few potatoes, part of the alms she had received during the day.

Half a dozen nearly naked children were lying on heaps of straw, pell-mell with a pig, a dog, a cat, two hens, and a duck. Never in my life had I seen such a hideous spectacle. The poor woman told me that her husband was a sailor, that he had gone to sea three years ago, and that she had not heard a word from him since.

She spread a mat on a box, the only piece of furniture in the house, and invited me to rest on it. The rain was falling in torrents, I knew not where to go, and I accepted the offer and placed myself on this hard bed of misfortune. The animals saluted, with loud cries, the first rays of the sun, and immediately began to hunt through the apartment for something to satisfy their devouring hunger.

The novelty of the situation was so singular as to amuse me for a moment, and after I felt as if transported to the ark, and believed myself to be Noah.

I must have appeared as extraordinary to the poor beasts as they appeared to me. The dog came and smelt me all over, showing his teeth; the pig examined me, grumbling the while; the hens and the duck devoured my powder puff; the children laughed; and I made haste to decamp before I should be myself devoured. I should add that I had a great deal of trouble to get my poor hostess to accept a miserable shilling.

DE LATOCHAYE, *A Frenchman's Walk Through Ireland*

It was at the middle one [cove] we had dinner in a cabin, potatoes and fairly good fish caught before our eyes from the rocks by children using pins for hooks. In order to cook our dinner the good woman had to crouch over the fire the whole time putting sea-rushes under the pot, for she had no other fuel. They also have fresh eggs (the hens nesting in a hole under the ground), a pig, a wooden cradle and a bed beside the fire in an enclosure of planks. The smoke passes out through the door. A beggar arrived to share the same roof who on being given potatoes began a long prayer all in Irish for the people of the house. I noticed here, as I have often noticed before, with what vigour the Irish express their gratitude. A gift of two shillings has earned me an infinite number of blessings.

CHARLES ETIENNE COGUEBERT DE MONTBRET,
Journal of Cork Historical and Archaeological Society

THE WAKE

Shaun Liam was moving around with a bottle of whisky and a glass. First he poured out a half-glass for Maura Tigue. Kate Joseph blushed and smiled as she saw the whisky approaching. She put a question to my grandfather, then glanced at the bottle without heeding his reply. Maura Tigue drained the glass.

'Well, dear God bless her soul and the souls of all the dead!' said she.

'Amen,' said we all.

I was still watching Kate Joseph. I could not but laugh inside my heart. As the bottle approached, a sharp look came into her eyes. She kept fidgeting anxiously in her corner. Shaun had not half filled the glass for her when, 'That's enough, Shaun, my lad,' said she; 'don't fill it right up. Ah, that's too much!'

She took a long draught of it, then coughed, and coughed again.

'You are choked with it,' said my grandfather.

'It is pretty strong enough,' said she, and you could hardly have heard her at the hole of your ear, for the drink had gone with her breath. With the second breath she tossed it all off and gave the blessing to the soul of old Kate as was meet. Then my grandfather drank a glass and, faith, I got a half one myself and drank it as well as anyone. Maura Tigue pulled out her pipe again and it passed from woman to woman till the room was full of smoke.

They were talking and smoking, my grandfather telling them of the great day they had at the Cosh long ago, when Mickil beat all the men of the place with his singing, till Shaun Liam came in again with a bucket of porter.

'Now,' said he, 'take a pull out of that.'

They were not slow to obey him, and the woman who was sitting shyly without a word till then was now warming up in wordy dispute with her neighbour, and my grandfather as merry as any.

I got up and went down to the kitchen. A big table was laid in the middle of the floor, five or six eating, talk throughout the house, a pipe in every mouth, the young keeping each other company in one corner and the old in another discussing seriously the affairs of the world. I threw myself among my equals, but I soon grew sick of their senseless chatter. I liked better the conversation of the old and that has been the way with me always, so I went up to the room again where I found the others as before.

After a while my grandfather got up and looked out through the window. 'Faith,' said he, 'the day is dawning. We had better go home, in the name of God.'

'Arra, musha, you know it is not day yet, Owen,' said Kate Joseph.

I wanted no more than the wind of the word, for I was blind with the sleep.

'Good night to you all,' said he.

'May the night prosper with you,' said the old women together.

'Upon my soul,' said my grandfather as we left the house, 'those women don't know that it isn't a wedding feast.'

MAURICE O'SULLIVAN, *Twenty Years A-Growing*

THERE IS A ROAD LOVE
LEADS US ON

WHEN YOU ARE OLD

When you are old and grey and full of sleep,
And nodding by the fire, take down this book,
And slowly read, and dream of the soft look
Your eyes had once, and of their shadows deep.

How many loved your moments of glad grace,
And loved your beauty with love false or true,
But one man loved the pilgrim soul in you,
And loved the sorrows of your changing face;

And bending down beside the glowing bars,
Murmur, a little sadly, how Love fled
And paced upon the mountains overhead
And hid his face amid a crowd of stars.

W. B. YEATS, Collected Poems

They came from Finn the king of Leinster, Rus Ruad's son, to woo me, and from Coirpre Niafer the king of Temair, another of Rus Ruad's sons. They came from Conchobor, king of Ulster, son of Fachtna, and they came from Eochaid Bec, and I wouldn't go. For I asked a harder wedding gift than any woman ever asked before from a man in Ireland – the absence of meanness and jealousy and fear.

'If I married a mean man our union would be wrong, because I'm so full of grace and giving. It would be an insult if I were more generous than my husband, but not if the two of us were equal in this. If my husband was a timid man our union would be just as wrong because I thrive, myself, on all kinds of trouble. It is an insult for a wife to be more spirited than her husband, but not if the two are equally spirited. If I married a jealous man that would be wrong, too: I never had one man without another waiting in his shadow. So I got the kind of man I wanted: Rus Ruad's other son – yourself, Ailill, from Leinster. You aren't greedy or jealous or sluggish. When we were promised, I brought you the best wedding gift a bride can bring: apparel enough for a dozen men, a chariot worth thrice seven bondmaids, the width of your face of red gold and the weight of your left arm of light gold. So, if anyone causes you shame or upset or trouble, the right to compensation is mine,' Medb said, 'for you're a kept man.'

'By no means,' Ailill said, 'but with the two kings for my brothers, Coirpre in Temair and Finn over Leinster. I let them rule because they were older, not because they are better than I am in grace or giving. I never heard, in all Ireland, of a province run by a woman except this one, which is why I came and took the kingship here, in succession to my mother Mata Muiresc, Mágach's daughter. Who better for my queen than you, a daughter of the high king of Ireland!

'It still remains,' Medb said, 'that my fortune is greater than yours.'

'You amaze me,' Ailill said. 'No one has more property or jewels or precious things than I have, and I know it.'

Then the lowliest of their possessions were brought out, to see who had more property and jewels and precious things: their buckets and tubs and iron pots, jugs and wash-pails and vessels with handles. Then their finger-rings, bracelets, thumb-rings and gold treasures were brought out, and their cloth of purple, blue, black, green and yellow, plain grey and many-coloured, yellow-brown, checked and striped. Their herds of sheep were taken in off the fields and meadows and plains. They were measured and matched, and found to be the same in numbers and size. Even the great ram leading Medb's sheep, the worth of one bondmaid by himself, had a ram to match him leading Ailill's sheep.

(Trans.) THOMAS KINSELLA, *The Táin*

IF I WERE TO GO WEST

If I were to go west, it is from the west I would not
    come,
On the hill that was highest, 'tis on it I would stand,
It is the fragrant branch I would soonest pluck,
And it is my own love I would quickest follow.

My heart is as black as a sloe,
Or as a black coal that would be burning in a forge,
As the sole of a shoe upon white halls,
And there is great melancholy over my laugh.

My heart is bruised, broken,
Like ice upon the top of water,
As it were a cluster of nuts after breaking,
Or a young maiden after her marrying.

My love is of the colour of the blackberries,
And the colour of the raspberry on a fine sunny day.
Of the colour of the darkest heath-berries of the
     mountain,
And often has there been a black head upon a bright
     body.

Time it is for me to leave this town,
The stone is sharp in it, and the mould is cold;
It was in it I got a voice without riches,
And a heavy word from the band who back-bite.

I denounce love; woe is she who gave it
To the son of you woman, who never understood it.
My heart in my middle, sure he has left it black,
And I do not see him on the street or in any place.
       DOUGLAS HYDE, *Studies and Translations from the Irish*

WOMAN FULL OF WILES

Oh woman full of wiles,
Keep away from me thy hand,
I am not a man for these things,
Though thou art sick for my love.

Do not think me perverse,
Do not bend thy head,
Let our love be inactive
Forever, oh slender fairy.
    GEOFFREY KEATING, (Trans. J. M. Synge in *Prose Works*)

PEGEEN *radiantly, wiping his face with her shawl*: Well, you're the lad, and you'll have great times from this out when you could win that wealth of prizes, and you sweating in the heat of noon!

CHRISTY *looking at her with delight*: I'll have great times if I win the crowning prize I'm seeking now, and that's your promise that you'll wed me in a fortnight, when our banns is called.

PEGEEN *backing away from him*: You've right daring to go ask me that, when all knows you'll be starting to some girl in your own townland, when your father's rotten in four months, or five.

CHRISTY *indignantly*: Starting from you, is it? *He follows her.* I will not, then, and when the airs is warming, in four months or five, it's then yourself and me should be pacing Neifin in the dews of night, the times sweet smells do be rising, and you'd see a little, shiny, new moon, maybe sinking on the hills.

PEGEEN *looking at him playfully*: And it's that kind of a poacher's love you'd make, Christy Mahon, on the sides of Neifin, when the night is down?

CHRISTY: It's little you'll think if my love's a poacher's, or an earl's itself, when you'll feel my two hands stretched around you, and I squeezing kisses on your puckered lips, till I'd feel a kind of pity for the Lord God is all ages sitting lonesome in His golden chair.

PEGEEN: That'll be right fun, Christy Mahon, and any girl would walk her heart out before she'd meet a young man was your like for eloquence, or talk at all.

CHRISTY *encouraged*: Let you wait, to hear me talking, till we're astray in Erris, when Good Friday's by, drinking a sup from a well, and making mighty kisses with our wetted mouths, or gaming in a gap of sunshine, with yourself stretched back unto your necklace, in the flowers of the earth.

PEGEEN *in a low voice, moved by his tone*: I'd be nice so, is it?

CHRISTY *with rapture*: If the mitred bishops seen you that time, they'd be the like of the holy prophets, I'm thinking, do be straining the bars of Paradise to lay eyes on the Lady Helen of Troy, and she abroad, pacing back and forward, with a nosegay in her golden shawl.

PEGEEN *with real tenderness*: And what is it I have, Christy Mahon, to make me fitting entertainment for the like of you, that has such poet's talking, and such bravery of heart.

CHRISTY *in a low voice*: Isn't there the light of seven heavens in your heart alone, the way you'll be an angel's lamp to me from this out, and I abroad in the darkness, spearing salmons in the Owen or the Carrowmore?

PEGEEN: If I was your wife I'd be along with you those nights, Christy Mahon, the way you'd see I was a great hand at coaxing bailiffs, or coining funny nicknames for the stars of night.

CHRISTY: You, is it? Taking your death in the hailstones, or in the fogs of dawn.

PEGEEN: Yourself and me would shelter easy in a narrow bush (*with a qualm of dread*); but we're only talking, maybe, for this would be a poor, thatched place to hold a fine lad is the like of you.

CHRISTY *putting his arm round her*: If I wasn't a good Christian, it's on my naked knees I'd be saying my prayers and paters to every jackstraw you have roofing your head, and every stony pebble is paving the laneway to your door.

PEGEEN *radiantly*: If that's the truth I'll be burning candles from this out to the miracles of God that have brought you from the south to-day, and I with my gowns bought ready, the way that I can wed you, and not wait at all.

CHRISTY: It's miracles, and that's the truth. Me there toiling a long while, and walking a long while, not knowing at all I was drawing all times nearer to this holy day.

PEGEEN: And myself, a girl, was tempted often to go sailing the seas till I'd marry a Jew-man, with ten kegs of gold, and I not knowing at all there was the like of you drawing nearer, like the stars of God.

CHRISTY: And to think I'm long years hearing women talking that talk, to all bloody fools, and this the first time I've heard the like of your voice talking sweetly for my own delight.

PEGEEN: And to think it's me is talking sweetly, Christy Mahon, and I the fright of seven townlands for my biting tongue. Well, the heart's a wonder; and, I'm thinking, there won't be our like in Mayo, for gallant lovers, from this hour to-day.

J. M. SYNGE, Playboy of the Western World

I now know that when a married woman says, 'Do come along – *he* certainly won't mind,' it's time for third parties to take to the woods.

This is knowledge, however, to be gained only in the hard school of life. It had not yet come my way when Suzanne Talbot suggested that they should put me up for the night.

There was no denying that some small emotional feeling had arisen between us during the Hunt Ball, warmed, no doubt, on Suzanne's part by the fact that her husband, Herbert, had spent the whole evening cementing a deal in cattle with three heavy men from Ballinasloe.

'But what,' I said, 'will the dashing rancher feel about it?'

'He,' said Suzanne, with the faintest, contemptuous emphasis, 'certainly won't mind.'

I guessed she was telling me that Herbert's life was bounded on all sides by cows, leaving him no time to consider the fact that his wife was only thirty-seven.

'It would save me,' I admitted, 'a long drive home.' She was a pretty little thing, somewhat crushed by the rigours of Irish country life. 'We might,' I said, 'have some further conversation about art, music, and letters.'

'You don't know what it's like,' she said with sudden passion, 'not to have to talk about hairball, footrot, and hookworm.' She dropped my hand. Herbert was on his way across the room.

'You ready, Annie?' he said. He nodded uncomfortably towards me. 'Hello, Mick –' he said. Herbert was certainly short of social graces. We had already been introduced. He might have tried to get a little closer to it than Mick.

'I'll get my things,' Suzanne said. 'I'll meet you in the hall.'

Herbert and I looked at the floor. I thought it would be unwise to tell him I was coming back for the night. Suzanne could do that in the car.

'Well, cheers,' said Herbert – 'look after yourself.' He slouched away.

I followed them home at a safe distance. Herbert, rigid in a boiled shirt, looked to me like a man who was ready for bed, but nonetheless I wanted to give him plenty of time to get tucked away.

146

He was waiting for me at the front door as I drove up. It was raining, but he came out on to the avenue in his shirt sleeves. 'Here,' he said, 'what sort of a game is this? Annie says you're staying the night.' His powerful face was knotted. A proposition had been made to him which passed his comprehension. 'You're a Dublin fella, aren't you?' said Herbert. 'What's stopping you going home?'

'Herbie!' cried Suzanne, 'whatever will Mr Campbell think of our manners?' She opened the door of my car. 'Do come in,' she said – 'have a drink – it's not so late –'

'Well,' I said – 'I'll just have one –'

Herbert crowded me enough to make it embarrassing to get out of the car. 'Here –' he said, protestingly, and then followed me, right on my heels, into the house.

There was no doubt that the situation had undergone a change. As a man who didn't mind Herbert was under false colours. And it no longer seemed important for me to brighten the life of his wife.

Suzanne threw open the sitting room door. 'You have your friends,' she told Herbert angrily, 'I don't see why I shouldn't have mine. Sit down and have a drink – darling,' she added, 'and I'll get your bed ready.'

She was merely being defiant. It was probably the first time in her life she had turned on him. But Herbert, a simple man, took the words at their face value.

'By God,' said Herbert, 'there'll be none of that!' Resolutely, he walked across the room and picked up a shotgun, which was leaning, surprisingly enough, against the desk.

I felt for the handle of the door. 'There is no need for us to behave like savages,' I said.

Herbert pulled out the top drawer of the desk, and broke open the gun. I knew he couldn't possibly be going to shoot, but still – if he loaded the thing – it might go off in his hand . . .

'Good night all,' I said, 'and thank you for a wonderful time.' I was in the car a moment later, driving hard down the avenue, waiting for the shots to crash round my ears.

What did crash round my ears, three miles farther on, was a soft little sigh, followed by a sort of plopping noise. I swung round in sudden terror. The back seat was occupied in its entirety by a large black dog – a labrador, by the look of it, waking from a deep sleep!

I stopped the car. I opened the back door. The dog looked at me heavily. It was not yet fully conscious. I examined the label round its neck.

ROGO

My first instinct was to put Rogo out into the night, and leave him to find his own way home. But Rogo looked much too large to walk three miles, even if he did happen to know the way. I decided to take him back to Herbert's gate, and leave the rest to his own good sense.

I coasted up to the gate, with the engine switched off, and left the car a little beyond it, under the shelter of a tree. I didn't know if the Talbots had gone to bed, but I did know that I had no further desire to meet them personally.

I lifted Rogo out of the back seat. He felt exactly like a fat woman in a fur coat. 'Good boy,' I said, 'go home.' It was still raining. Rogo shivered and slowly climbed back into the car again. I tried to stop him, seizing him round his large waist, but he snarled so fiercely I had to let him go.

I got the starting-handle from the boot and tried to prod him out on to the road. The handle sank horribly into his large and yielding flank, but Rogo refused to move.

I started to bark softly, waving my hands about in the dim light of the dashboard lamp. I thought the disturbance might cause the dog to rise to his feet, and then I could suddenly push him out while he was off-balance.

I was absolutely astonished to see the face of a policeman looking in through the open door.

'Well, hello,' I said, after a moment, 'I was trying to get this damn dog out of the car.' Then, I said, 'You're out very late. Are you looking for murderers?' I wanted to remind him that he probably had some more important job to do.

He came round to my side, a young policeman like a bullock, probably a native Irish speaker if given a chance to gather his wits.

He looked at me cautiously. 'It's not in me powers,' he said, 'to acquaint the civilian population with the nature of me duties. Is this your dog?'

'Well, no,' I said, 'it belongs to Mr Talbot up at the house. I'm trying to get him to go home.'

'And what,' he said, 'is the animal doin' out of the owner's jurisdiction at this hour of the night?'

'I drove it away, by mistake,' I said. 'It got into the back of the car by itself and now I can't get it out.'

There was a long, baffled silence.

'I'll have to ask you,' said the young policeman, 'to proceed up to the premises. You'll be drivin' the vehicle,' he added. He was not going to take the risk of being shot in the back.

We drove slowly up the avenue. The policeman seemed to occupy three-quarters of the front seat. Rogo took up the whole of the back. I had fled lightly from the Talbots. I was returning to them laden down to the scuppers.

The policeman got out. 'As a matter of precaution,' he said to me, 'I'll have to ask you to dismount.' I joined him on the doorstep. He seized the knocker. A thunderous sound rang through the darkened house.

'Bad old class of a night,' said the policeman, in a conversational tone. I told him I'd never known worse. Then the door opened and Herbert, in a dressing-gown, stood on the threshold. The policeman must have been accustomed to rousing people from their beds. He paid no attention to Herbert's suffused face.

'It's me duty, sir,' he said, 'to make official enquiries into the ownership of an animal found in this gintleman's motor vehicle. The gintleman is making allegations that the animal belongs to you.'

Herbert saw me for the first time. He took a pace forward. 'You've taken my *dog*!' he exclaimed. He meant that I'd settled for his dog, having failed to take his wife.

'It got into the back of the car,' I snapped. 'I didn't want any part of it.'

Herbert looked. 'Where is it?' he said.

The back seat was empty. Rogo had gone back to bed, no doubt sensing that he was home again, after an inexplicable interruption.

'Holy fly,' said the policeman, 'an' wasn't it only lookin' at me a minit ago.'

'A black overgrown thing,' I said crossly. The policeman seemed to think a miracle had happened. 'It was called Rogo. It was there all right.'

'That's my dog,' said Herbert. 'I wouldn't lose that dog for a fortune.' Suddenly he wanted to get hold of one concrete fact. 'I'm going to see if that dog's in his kennel,' he announced, 'and if he isn't –' He made a wild gesture. He didn't know what would happen after that.

We followed him round to the yard. Rogo was at home, fast asleep in a kennel the size of a block of flats.

'Well,' I said, 'are you satisfied now?'

Herbert looked round heavily. 'With what?' he said.

I'd had enough. 'Officer,' I said. 'We're going home. You can issue the summonses in the morning.' It really didn't matter what anyone was talking about any more.

I drove him into the village and left him outside the police station. He seemed surprised I wouldn't come in. 'I've all me reports to do about the occurrence,' he complained. 'The sergeant is the divil an' all for writin' . . .'

I drove off abruptly without saying good-bye. I must have gone less than a mile when a voice said, 'Guess who's here.' It was a subdued and wary voice, and it came from the back seat.

I had no difficulty in identifying it as the voice of Suzanne, the lovely wife of Herbert Talbot, cattle dealer, of Grange House, Westmeath.

I stopped the car. With a weary sense of repetition, I went round to get the starting-handle out of the boot.

PATRICK CAMPBELL, *Thirty-five Years on the Job*

THE ONLY JEALOUSY OF EMER

Cuchulain stopped a month in that country with Fand, and at the end of the month he bade her farewell, and she said to him: 'In whatever place you tell me to go and meet you, I will go there.' And the place they settled to meet at was at Ibar Cinn Tracta, the yew at the head of Baile's strand.

But when all this was told to Emer, there was great anger on her, and she had knives made ready to kill the woman with; and she came, and fifty young girls with her, to the place where they had settled to meet.

Cuchulain and Laeg were playing chess there, and they did

not see the women coming. It was Fand saw them first, and she said to Laeg: 'Look, Laeg, at what I see.' 'What is that?' said Laeg. Then he looked, and it is what Fand said: 'Look behind you, Laeg; there are women listening to you, wise, with sharp, green knives in their right hands, with gold at their well-shaped breasts; they move as brave men do, going through a battle of chariots. Well does Emer, daughter of Forgall, change colour in her anger.'

'No harm shall be done to you by her,' said Cuchulain; 'and she shall not reach to you at all. Come into the sunny seat of the chariot, opposite myself, for I will defend you against all the many women of the four points of Ulster; for though Forgall's daughter may threaten,' he said, 'on the strength of her companions, to do some daring thing, it is surely not against me she will dare it.'

Then Cuchulain said to Emer: 'It is little I mind you, woman, in spite of my affection for you, more than any other man minds a woman. The spear in your shaking hand does not wound me, nor your weak, thin knife, nor your vain, gathered anger; for it would be a pity my strength to be put down by a woman's strength.'

'I ask then,' said Emer, 'what was it led you, Cuchulain, to dishonour me before all the women of the province, and before all the women of Ireland, and before all honourable people in the same way? For it was under your shelter I came, and on the strength of your faithfulness; for although you threaten a great quarrel in your pride, it is certain, Cuchulain, you cannot put me away, even if you would try to do it.'

'I ask you, Emer,' said Cuchulain, 'why I may not have my turn in the company of this woman; for in the first place she is well-behaved, comely, well-mannered, worthy of a king, this woman from beyond the waves of the great sea; with form and countenance and high descent; with embroidery and handiness, with sense and quickness; for there is not anything under the skies her husband could ask, but she would do it, even if she had not given her promise. And O Emer,' he said, 'you will never find any brave, comely man so good as myself.'

'It is certain,' said Emer, 'that I will not refuse this woman if you follow her. But all the same, everything red is beautiful, everything new is fair, everything high is lovely, everything common is bitter, everything we are without is thought much of, everything we know is thought little of, till all knowledge is known. And O Cuchulain,' she said, 'I was at one time in esteem with you and I would be so again, if it were pleasing to you.'

And grief came upon her, and overcame her. 'By my word, now,' said Cuchulain, 'you are pleasing to me, and will be pleasing as long as I live.'

'Let me be given up,' said Fand. 'It is better for me to be given up,' said Emer. 'Not so,' said Fand, 'it is I that will be given up in the end, and it is I that have been in danger of it all this time.'

And great grief and trouble of mind came to Fand, because she was ashamed to be given up, and to have to go back to her home there and then; and the great love she had given Cuchulain troubled her; and so she was lamenting, and she made this complaint:

'It is I will go on the journey; I agree to it with great sorrow; though my father has so great a name, I would sooner stay with Cuchulain. It would be better for me to be here, to be under your rule without grief, than to go, though you may wonder at it, to the sunny house of Aedh Abrat.

'O Emer, the man is yours, and well may you wear him, for you are worthy; what my arm cannot reach, that at least I may wish well to.

'Many were the men asking for me, in the court and in country places; I never went to meet one of them, for it is myself was of right behaviour.

'A pity it is to give love to a man, and he to take no heed to it. It is better to be turned away, if you are not loved as you love.'

LADY GREGORY, *Cuchulain of Muirthemne*

Walking by my side on that night of our first meeting after her release, along a lonely road high over the city, staring down at the lights far below, she said to me:

'You are all abstract fanatics. You are suffering, if you are suffering, not out of love for your fellow men but out of love for your own ruthless selves.'

It was more or less what Sean O'Casey was to say about all patriotism in his two great plays later on. Staring coldly at the valley's lights, I said that people who thought like that should be shot as traitors.

She said: 'Some morning you will wake up to find yourself standing in the Grand Parade behind a green iron railing holding up the torch of liberty, not a man at all but a statue made of stone or lead.'

After that those two young people walked on in silence beyond the last of the city's road lamps. They walked close together, full of affection, threatened by anger and by hate. I say 'they' because the whole of this thing is no longer with me as a matter of she and me. That 'she' and that 'me' exist now only as figures in a fiction, or a play printed on the sheets of memory, or ghosts that have left indelible imprints on a place they once frequented in passion. I see him and her walking home full of unhappiness at the shattering of their dreams. They went on meeting one another only because their love and loyalty were stronger than Ireland or mankind.

SEAN O'FAOLAIN, *Vive Moi*

COURTING

The conversation opened in the normal way:
'Hello.'
'Hello, Tarry.'

The way she used his Christian name fluttered Tarry's heart to little blown bits like leaves in a wind. Her voice caressed him.

'I wasn't expecting you,' he said.

She just looked at him as she had looked once before, and he was quite helpless. But not completely. Automatically he said in a super-objective manner: 'I was just thinking of going up this old road when you came –'

They walked, threading their way among the bushes and briars and over rabbit burrows and the greasy stumps of long-felled trees.

'Marvellous weather,' said he with all the passion of a lover.
'Terrific,' she said.

'Look at the rabbit,' he said, continuing his love talk. 'Give me your hand and I'll give you a pull over that gripe.'

He pulled on her hand and having landed her over the soaking trench let go of her hand. He felt that it was up to him as an honourable man not to get a set-in in that way. Afterwards he was mad with himself. It would be much harder to make a second attempt.

They climbed up the hill and through a narrow gap which looked north over Miskin and away down through the dark valleys of Lisdoonan. Almost below them in the hollow was the Parochial House. Father Daly was walking through the field beside the river carrying a golf club on his shoulder.

'You were often in the Parochial House?' he said. 'I never was.'

He did not wait for a reply to this but hurried on to talk about the crops and more weather lore.

'Aren't them nettles very vicious looking?' she said.

He delivered a short lecture on the various kinds of nettles. The sun slanted low and the song of the blackbird thrilled the evening. To the left of them below they could see Petey Meegan come from behind a hay-stack buttoning his trousers. A moment later he was seen putting the lock on his door and dragging himself over the fence as he went on his way to Flynn's. At the same moment they could hear the voice of Tarry's sister, Mary, whispering to her town lover among the briars below them.

A corncrake screeched in Kerley's hay field. In the distance could be heard the rattle of tin cans being left down on stones outside some door. Some woman's voice came across the valleys: 'Drive them calves to the field, Joe.'

'That's a clouting evening for the spuds,' said Tarry.

'Do you think so, Tarry?' the girl said. 'Sit down here.'

He found himself sitting beside her. But he was ill at ease. One part of his mind told him to run, that to be great he must run away from things like this. He knew it was fear, a deep instinct that he could never hope to hold this girl.

Through the bushes he could see the corner of one of his new fields and the sight shamed him when he compared it with the broad tree-lined fields of Reilly's which spread out in the distance.

'I think your new farm is wonderful,' she said as if knowing his mind. 'Here, sit on the tail of this coat.' She spread her coat on the dewy grass and now he was sitting closer than ever he had sat to a girl before. And it was the girl he had dreamt of. He was terribly unhappy, thinking of an hour ahead when it would be all over. Now he was in the company of one who belonged to the highest society of the parish. What would Eusebius say? He would try to make a jeer of it, for that was the kind of Eusebius.

Mary Reilly was so different from Molly who had twisted his thumb and left him more exhausted after his struggle with her than he would be after a day's mowing with a scythe or a day carrying a knapsack sprayer.

She twisted a briar that hung over his head and wound it round a whin root.

'It's a powerful evening,' said he.

He had his hand on the bank behind her within one inch of her back. He would give a good deal to have the courage to move his hand one inch. Eventually he took his hand away altogether.

'You must come up to our house some evening,' she suggested.

'Oh, God! no,' he cried, the offer being too good to be true. 'Sure Father Markey and everybody does be up there.'

'What harm?'

'Oh, I don't know,' he said petulantly.

'You must make a poem for me some day, Tarry.'

He shook his head from side to side. 'Sure I do only be at that for a cod.'

'My! Father Markey thinks you great.'

Tarry was afraid to hear more on that subject though at the time he did not know the reason.

'Were you never talking to him?' she asked.

'I never was talking to a priest in me life,' he said truthfully.

'He has a brother who writes plays,' said she.

'Holies!'

The girl had shut her eyes softly and was leaning her head towards Tarry. Tarry instead of yielding stiffened himself and she straightened up. 'We'd better be getting back,' she said.

They passed Mary Flynn and her lover in the briars as they

155

came down the hill. The girl went round by the main road on her way home. Tarry, talking to himself, walked home alone.

PATRICK KAVANAGH, *Tarry Flynn*

At mid-day gay sweet-voiced Maraed de Barra, myself and another person went to Desart Court along the same way I went on Easter Sunday. We walked through the dark ever-green pine woods where we were sheltered from the sun as we went along the fine winding paths which straightened out now and again. We could hear the lark's song in the nearby meadows, the shorter call of the blackbird, the thrush and all the smaller birds which seemed to be in harmony with Maraed de Barra's gentle lively melodious speech. We went astray in a dark shadowy little glen until we couldn't make out east from west or north from south. At long last, having gone through mossy hollows, clumps of brambles, slopes covered with ash trees, and evergreen pine groves, we reached Cluain Lachan with its ponds, pools, lakelets, streams and murmuring waterfalls. White ducks and spotted drakes were there, and the blackbirds were singing to each other in the bush-tops. 'I am tired,' said sweet gentle vivacious Maraed. 'So am I.' 'Let us sit down on the moss-covered rock.' 'Certainly.' Maraed dozed off to sleep with the murmuring of the waterfall. 'Croon wind, through the trees in the swamp. Don't blow noisily or threateningly!' The wind blew gently through the sleeping wanderer's hair and laid bare her neck as white as the swan on the lake. Her little lips were as red as the rowan and as sweet as honey. Her breasts like two snow-clad knolls rose and fell like the swell on the King's River. Her neat little buttocks and her pretty little legs were hidden by her satin dress, down to her small tidy feet. Two snipe flew off from a pool near us like arrows from a bow. My beautiful young lady started from her sound sleep. 'May there be no pool for you in Ireland ever again,' said I. 'May there not be.' 'The sun is setting. Let us be off home.' We went off, tired and weary, her arm in mine, her head on my shoulder, her eyes lowered to the ground. I never remember a more pleasant day.

The Diary of Humphrey O'Sullivan (1828) (Trans. Thomas de Bhaldraith)

THE RED-HAIRED MAN'S WIFE

I have taken that vow –
   And you were my friend
But yesterday – now
   All that's at an end,
And you are my husband, and claim me, and I
   must depend.

Yesterday I was free,
   Now you, as I stand,
Walk over to me
   And take hold of my hand.
You look at my lips, your eyes are too bold,
   your smile is too bland.

My old name is lost,
   My distinction of race:
Now the line has been crossed,
   Must I step to your pace?
Must I walk as you list, and obey, and smile up
   in your face?

All the white and the red
   Of my cheeks you have won;
All the hair of my head,
   And my feet, tho' they run,
Are yours, and you own me and end me just as
   I begun.

JAMES STEPHENS

LABASHEEDY (THE SILKEN BED)

I'd make a bed for you
in Labasheedy
in the tall grass
under the wrestling trees
where your skin
would be silk
in the darkness
when the moths are coming down.

Skin which glistens
shining over your limbs
like milk being poured
from jugs at dinnertime;
your hair is a herd of goats
moving over rolling hills,
hills that have high cliffs
and two ravines.

And your damp lips
would be as sweet as sugar
at evening and we walking
by the riverside
with honeyed breezes
blowing over the Shannon
and the fuchsias bowing down to you
one by one.

The fuchsias bending low
their folemn heads in obeisance to the beauty
in front of them
I would pick a pair of flowers
as pendant earrings
to adorn you
like a bride in shining clothes.

O I'd make a bed for you
in Labasheedy,
in the twilight hour
with evening falling slow
and what a pleasure it would be
to have our limbs entwine
wrestling
while the moths are coming down.

NUALA NI DHOMHNAILL, Selected Poems

COUNTRY MARRIAGE

A match usually begins when a farmer casts round for a suitable wife for one of his sons. The son to be married is to inherit the farm. The farmer has full power to choose among his sons. A hundred years ago, before famine, clearances and land reform, all the sons and daughters could hope to be provided for on the land. Such a situation is still an ideal, but little more. One cannot subdivide one's holding any longer, and new farms are hard to get. Today the farmer looks forward, ordinarily, to 'settling' only one son 'on the land'.

'The young man,' the farmer goes on, 'sends a "speaker" to the young lady and the speaker will sound a note to know what fortune she has, will she suit, and will she marry this Shrove? She and her friends will inquire what kind of a man he is, is he nice and steady. And if he suits, they tell the speaker to go ahead and "draw it down". So then he goes back to the young man's house and arranges for them to meet in such a place, on such a night and we will see about it.' With this, the first step in the delicate negotiations is safely passed.

The Inagh farmer goes on: 'The speaker goes with the young man and his father that night, and they meet the father of the girl and his friends or maybe his son and son-in-law. The first drink is called by the young man; the second by the young lady's father.

'The young lady's father asks the speaker what fortune do he want. He asks him the place of how many cows, sheep, and horses is it? He asks what makings of a garden are in it; is there plenty of water or spring wells? Is it far in from the road, or on it? What kind of house is in it, slate or thatch? Are the cabins good, are they slate or thatch? If it is too far in from the road, he won't take it. Backward places don't grow big fortunes. And he asks, too, is it near a chapel and the school, or near town?'

The Inagh countryman could pause here; he had summarized a very long and important negotiation.

'Well,' he went on, getting to the heart of the matter, 'if it is a nice place, near the road, and the place of eight cows, they are sure to ask £350 fortune. Then the young lady's father offers £250. Then maybe the boy's father throws off £50. If the young lady's father still has £250 on it, the speaker divides the £50 between them. So now it's £275. Then the young man says he is not willing to marry without £300 – but if she's a nice girl and a good housekeeper, he'll think of it. So, there's another drink by the young man, and then another by the young lady's father, and so on with every second drink till they're near drunk. The speaker gets plenty and has a good day.'

The farmer paused here again; for the match is developing marvellously. 'All this is one day's work,' he continued. 'After this, they appoint a place for the young people to see one another and be introduced. The young lady takes along her friends, maybe another girl, and her brother and her father and mother. The young man takes along his friends and the speaker.

'If they suit one another, then they will appoint a day to come and see the land. If they don't, no one will reflect on anybody, but they will say he or she doesn't suit. They do not say plainly what is wrong.

'The day before the girl's people come to see the land, geese are killed, the house is whitewashed, whiskey and porter bought. The cows get a feed early so as to look good; and maybe they get an extra cow in, if they want one.' He said this last slyly, for to pretend to own more stock than one really has, is an unfair trick in the bargaining.

'Then next day comes the walking of the land. The young man stays outside in the street, but he sends his best friend in to show the girl's father round, but sure the friend won't show him the bad points.

'If the girl's father likes the land he returns, and there will be eating and drinking until night comes on them. Then they go to an attorney next day and get the writings between the two parties and get the father of the boy to sign over the land.' With the writings, the match is made, and the wedding can go forward.

CONRAD ARENSBERG, *The Irish Countryman*

GATEPOSTS

A man will keep a horse for prestige,
But a woman ripens best underground.
He settles where the wind
Brings his whirling hat to rest,
And the wind decides which door is to be used.

Under the hip-roofed thatch,
The bed-wing is warmed by the chimney breast;
On either side the keeping-holes
For his belongings, hers.

He says it's unlucky to widen the house,
And leaves the gateposts holding up the fairies.
He lays his lazy-beds and burns the river,
He builds turf-castles,
And sprigs the corn with apple-mint.

She spreads heather on the floor
And sifts the oatmeal ark for thin-bread farls:
All through the blue month
She tosses stones in basins to the sun,
And watches for the trout in the holy well.

MEDBH MCGUCKIAN, *Marconi's Cottage*

FOR ANNE GREGORY

'Never shall a young man,
Thrown into despair
By those great honey-coloured
Ramparts at your ear,
Love you for yourself alone
And not your yellow hair.'

'But I can get a hair-dye
And set such colour there,
Brown, or black, or carrot,
That young men in despair
May love me for myself alone
And not my yellow hair.'

'I heard an old religious man
But yesternight declare
That he had found a text to prove
That only God, my dear,
Could love you for yourself alone
And not your yellow hair.'

W. B. YEATS, *Collected Poems*

THERE'S A GIRL IN THIS TOWN

THE BOY.   There's a girl in this town,
            And her name it is Máire,
            I gave her love and liking
            Beyond all the girls of the place.
            I have no gold, I have no silver,
            Nor anything but my health,
            And if an empty man is your choice,
            You may have me and welcome.

162

THE GIRL. O young youth,
In whose pockets is the yellow gold,
That I may see your halls
Bright, and your coaches;
That I may see your garden
Full of every fruit,
And the hundreds dying
For desire of marrying you.

I thought, myself,
For I was without knowledge,
That you would give me your hand
Or the wedding-ring;
And I thought after that
That you were the star of knowledge,
Or the blossom of the strawberry
On each side of the boreen.

THE BOY.

I am a poor buachaillín
A-leaving Ireland,
Going into France
In the army of King James.
I sold my estate
For a quart of sour drink,
And, O my dear woman of the house,
Give me the wetting of my mouth.

THE GIRL. O young youth,
Who has the yellow gold in his ringlets,
And too many young women
Kissing your small mouth;
That I may never leave this world
Which is slanderous and lying
Until I rear your childeen
On the white bosom of my shirt.

DOUGLAS HYDE, *Studies and Translations from the Irish*

LOVERS ON ARAN

The timeless waves, bright sifting, broken glass,
Came dazzling around, into the rocks,
Came glinting, sifting from the Americas

To possess Aran. Or did Aran rush
To throw wide arms of rock around a tide
That yielded with an ebb, with a soft crash?

Did sea define the land or land the sea?
Each drew new meaning from the waves' collision.
Sea broke on land to full identity.

SEAMUS HEANEY, *Selected Poems*

THE CRY OF THE OLD KINGS

FIONN

He was a king, a seer, and a poet. He was a lord with a manifold and great train. He was our magician, our knowledgeable one, our soothsayer. All that he did was sweet with him. And, however ye deem my testimony of Fionn excessive, and, although ye hold my praising overstrained, nevertheless, and by the King that is above me, he was three times better than all I say.

SAINT PATRICK

THE BOYHOOD OF FIONN

Fionn got his first training among women. There is no wonder in that, for it is the pup's mother teaches it to fight, and women know that fighting is a necessary art although men pretend there are others that are better. These were the women druids, Bovmall and Lia Luachra.

It is likely the women were fond of him, for other than Fionn there was no life about them. He would be their life; and their eyes may have seemed as twin benedictions resting on the small fair head. He was fair-haired, and it was for his fairness that he was afterwards called Fionn; but at this period he was known as Deimne. They saw the food they put into his little frame reproduce itself lengthways and sideways in tough inches, and in springs and energies that crawled at first, and then toddled, and then ran. He had birds for playmates, but all the creatures that live in a wood must have been his comrades. There would have been for little Fionn long hours of lonely sunshine, when the world seemed just sunshine and a sky. There would have been hours as long, when existence passed like a shade among shadows, in the multitudinous tappings of rain that dripped from leaf to leaf in the wood, and slipped so to the ground. He would have known little snaky paths, narrow enough to be filled by his own small feet, or a goat's; and he would have wondered where they went, and have marvelled again to find that, wherever they went, they came at last, through loops and twists of the branchy wood, to his own door. He may have thought of his own door as the beginning and end of the world, whence all things went, and whither all things came.

JAMES STEPHENS, *Irish Fairy Tales*

BRICRU'S FEAST

'Have done with this word-fighting, lest you drive the men of Ulster to grow white-faced in the anger and the pride of battle with one another.

'It is through the fault of women the shields of men are broken, heroes go out to fight and struggle with one another in their anger.

'It is the folly of women brings men to do these things, to bruise what they cannot bind up again, to strike down what they cannot raise up again. Wives of heroes, keep yourself from this.'

But Emer answered him, and it is what she said:

'It is right for me to speak, Sencha, and I the wife of the comely, pleasant hero, who is beyond all others in beauty, in wisdom, in speaking, since the learning that was easy to him is done with.

'No one can do his feats, the over-breath feat, the apple feat, the ghost feat, the screw feat, the cat feat, the red-whirling feat, the barbed-spear feat, the quick stroke, the fire of the mouth, the hero's cry, the wheel feat, the sword-edge feat; no one can throw himself against hard-spiked places the way he does.

'There is no one is his equal in youth, in form, in brightness, in birth, in mind, in voice, in bravery, in boldness, in fire, in skill; no one is his equal in hunting, in running, in strength, in victories, in greatness. There is no man to be found who can be put beside Cuchulain.'

LADY GREGORY, *Cuchulain of Muirthemne*

The maids did not get into the other world in the way we did who knew more about it. Although they were thankful for holy days and went to Mass, they were really more interested in an old Irish world where fairies, witches, and banshees took the place of our angels and saints. We children were forbidden to pry into that magic place which was, mother told us, imaginary and untrue, but we could not help knowing that the maids and most of the untaught people round Lough Gur believed that a third world, fraught with danger, was going on all round them. *God be between us and harm*, was for ever on their lips – if a red-haired stranger came to the door; if a cock crowed during the day; if a heedless girl swept the floor towards the door;* if she lit a candle without first crossing herself† or forgot to 'nip the cake'.‡

The powers of evil, always on the alert to entangle and destroy souls, being most dangerous and most powerful on May eve, on that day the maids were apt to be uneasy and rather sullen, watching us suspiciously lest we might, through our unbelief, frustrate their precautions against danger. They strewed primroses on the threshold of front and back doors – no fairy can get over this defence – and in the cow-byres they hung branches of rowan while the head dairywoman sprinkled holy water in mangers and stalls. The milkmaids, at the end of the evening milking, stood to make the sign of the cross with froth from the pails, signing themselves and making a cross in the air towards the cows.

Mother, who had been giving out the Rosary one May eve – it was the first after my return from school – lingered a little on the prayer for protection and added the words from the psalms:

> *If thou sleep thou shalt not fear,*
> *Thou shalt rest and thy sleep shall be sweet.*

It was as if she wished to re-assure the nervous maids.

Father got up from his knees and forgetting it was May eve

* This sends good luck from the house.
† To ward off evil spirits.
‡ Breaking a small piece from a newly-baked cake or loaf to avert bad luck.

he told Ellie to make up a good fire, for the crumley-cow* was sick and hot water might be needed.

Ellie and Bridgie looked at one another in consternation and went over to the hearth, where the fire was almost dead, to confer with Tom Hickey who was having supper, and to pity him for having to sit up all night beside the crumley-cow in the great danger of the byre.

' 'Tis a quare thing', Tom said in a low voice, 'that every cow in the byre has a bunch of primroses on her tail but just the one, the crumley, and she needing it the most, the crayther! I've a mind to singe her along the back with a wisp of straw.'†

'Ye c'ld do so when the masther's in his bed,' Ellie said.

'Will I make up a bunch for her tail?' Bridgie asked sympathetically. 'There's lashans of primroses yet in the coop where Ellie have them hid agin the tramplin' of the children on the doorstep.'

'God help them,' Ellie said, 'and them so bould agin the dangers of this night.' She crossed herself anxiously.

'God between us and harm,' Bridgie whispered, doing likewise.

' 'Tis not the *Good People* I'd be in dread of in the dark of night,' Tom told them, 'but to hear the cry of the Ould Kings.'

The maids shivered. 'God send they rest in their graves.'

MARY CARBERRY, The Farm by Lough Gur

THE CLURICAUNE

While the dark and stormy Phooka performs acts of desperate daring, whirling people from mountain to mountain, and then casting them into the deepest morass he can discover; while the elves, the legitimate moonlight fairies, sport in 'the rings', the woods, along the yellow sands, and through the halls of the olden time; while the lonely Banshee flits about the relics of old places, frighting the lone owl with the wail of death; the Cluricaune curls himself under a hedge to mend his tiny 'brogue'; seats himself astride a butt of the best wine in the

* Cow with crumpled horns.
† A potent charm against fairies.

cellar of a friend's house, and taps the juice of the grape for his own advantage; or, it may be, counts over the treasures which he loves to conceal in the caves of the earth, or among the stones that betoken past magnificence. In fine, while others of fairy land are more intent upon pastime and pleasure, the Cluricaune, Leprehaun, Lewricaun, or whatever you may please to call him, is intent upon business, and a quaint methodical enjoyment of the comforts of life, seasoned with a sprinkling of mischief to prevent insipidity. He has a decided preference for some families over others; for he will eat of their bread and drink of their cup as long as it continues to be supplied so as to suit his own ideas of respect and convenience; but if they neglect him, though he does not desert, he punishes them in return, and sometimes so severely, that his absence might be esteemed a favour; he is, moreover, an insolent little fellow – cutting and sarcastic – an elderly Puck, a systematic 'Robin-goodfellow'. In fact, the Irish Cluricaune seems to have monopolised the forethought of the country; and, as an old Irish gardener remarked to us, 'if he has a respect for anything in the world, it is for an ancient family – as long as it keeps a good cellar.'

MR AND MRS HALL, *Ireland: Scenery and Character 1825–40*

THE WEST ROOM

My host's house in Luogh was like the others. It was a bit 'stronger', that is, neater, better built and kept, than many of the others, but it was like the others in all essentials. It was a white-washed stone cottage, rectangular, roofed with slate (though it was only a few years ago that they gave up thatch). Its long sides faced roughly north and south, each with a door opening directly out into the yards. In the gable of the roof was a loft for sleeping; otherwise it was confined to a single story. The central room, the largest by far, was the kitchen. There the family passed their lives and prepared and ate the food cooked on the hearth. The hearth was an open turf fire, built in a chimney large enough to have two hobs or seats deep within on either side. It had, too, an iron hook which swung the cooking-pots out into the room from off the fire.

Behind this hearth was another room. It was called, for its position in the house, the 'west room'.

In most countrymen's houses, especially in poorer regions, the 'west room', that behind the hearth, is the only room except for the kitchen and the loft. In some houses, however, there is another room too. This is usually a bedroom, at the opposite end of the kitchen. This was the case at my host's.

But in either case it soon becomes apparent that there is something special about the west room. At Luogh this struck one's eye immediately. At my host's the room was a sort of parlour into which none but distinguished guests were admitted. In it were kept pictures of the dead and emigrated members of the family, all 'fine' pieces of furniture, symbolic brass objects brought in by the bride at marriage; the rubrics used when mass was celebrated in the house, in fact all religious objects, crucifixes, and so forth, except the 'blessed lamp' and a 'holy picture' in the kitchen. Nor were my hosts alone in keeping objects of sentimental and religious value in this special room. Other houses did likewise. The general feeling was that such objects 'belonged' there.

But these facts had little significance until others began to appear. Here we enter the realm which we ordinarily called 'old custom'. The 'west room' had still another association, of a supernatural cast. This appeared only gradually. The 'west room' was of central importance in fairy lore.

In this all Luogh concurred, though few could be found to give it expression. The cult of the fairies, these days, is branded as 'superstition'. It is under fire from townsman, schoolteacher, and priest. But even those who could express no views could be seen to act as if they too were believers.

Where fairy paths were remembered to pass the house, they went by the west room. Where food and water was left out at night, it was left there. No outhouse, shed, or other building could be built on this side of the house. That would bring bad luck. Very few could or would tell why; they left it to a common inference. The building would be 'in the way'. Nevertheless, reluctant as they might be to express belief, my hosts none the less practised it. No house of Luogh's twenty-six had any shed or outhouse at its western end.

CONRAD ARENSBERG, *The Irish Countryman*

GOING ASTRAY

When I opened the front door after dark that night there was one of the lambs nudging my knees like a dog. It followed me into the paddock and after shutting the gate I began to search for a hole in the fence. As I walked across towards the other side, I lost my way. I walked here and there and in circles for about two hours, sometimes sitting down to gather my wits, sometimes walking straight ahead, as I thought, but never reaching fence or wall, always wandering as though in endless space. I became frightened. At last I lay down on the grass. It was damp and cold. The lush smell of Ireland soaked me as it had on the day of my arrival eleven years before. I slept for a bit and when I woke walked straight back to the house without doubting the direction I took.

During the next few days I told several people about this experience. They laughed when they heard I had been led astray by a pet lamb. I mentioned my peculiar defect of eye-sight called night-blindness by the London oculist who said my pupils took hours to widen in the dark when other men's took seconds, which made me entirely blind whenever I left a lighted place for a dark one. But no one I spoke to took this for a reason. 'Going astray' was a common thing to them. Anyone who had not been astray knew someone else who had. Some said certain fields were known to have 'a stray' in them, meaning a lost soul I think. One man said you would be lost if you walked over the grave of an unbaptised baby and a very old man at Cootehall believed it could only happen in a 'gentle place'. He said the 'gentry' would put you astray.

DAVID THOMSON, *Woodbrook*

THE MONKEY

John FitzThomas FitzGerald (later to become the 1st Earl of Kildare in 1316) was born around 1250 and was heir to his uncle, Maurice, 5th Baron Offaly.

He was an infant in the Castle of Woodstock near Athy when there was an alarm of fire. In the confusion that ensued the children were forgotten and when the servants returned to search for him, the room in which he lay was found in ruins. Soon after a strange noise was heard in one of the towers and on looking up they saw an ape, which was usually kept chained, carefully holding the child in his arms (and which he brought down safely). The Earl afterwards in gratitude for his preservation, adopted a monkey for his crest and supporters. (The monkey in the coat of arms is seen with a collar and broken chain.)

From *The Earls of Kildare*

THE SIDHE

The Sidhe cannot make themselves visible to all. They are shape-changers; they can grow small or grow large, they can take what shape they choose; they appear as men or women wearing clothes of many colours, of today or of some old forgotten fashion, or they are seen as bird or beast, or as a barrel or a flock of wool. They go by us in a cloud of dust; they are as many as the blades of grass. They are everywhere; their home is in the forths, the lisses, the ancient round grass-grown mounds. There are thorn-bushes they gather near and protect; if they have a mind for a house like our own they will build it up in a moment. They will remake a stone castle, battered by Cromwell's men, if it takes their fancy, filling it with noise and lights. Their own country is Tir-nan-Og – the Country of the Young. It is under the ground or under the sea, or it may not be far from any of us. As to their food, they will use common things left for them on the hearth or outside the threshold, cold potatoes it may be, or a cup of water or of milk. But for their feasts they choose the best of all sorts, taking it from the solid world, leaving some worthless likeness in its place; when they rob the potatoes from the ridges the diggers find but rottenness and decay; they take the strength from the meat in the pot, so that when put on the plates it does not nourish. They will not touch salt; there is danger to them in it. They will go to good cellars to bring away the wine.

Fighting is heard among them, and music that is more beautiful than any of this world; they are seen dancing on the rocks; they are often seen playing at the hurling, hitting balls towards the goal. In each one of their households there is a queen, and she has more power than the rest; but the greatest power belongs to their fool, the Fool of the Forth, Amadan-na-Briona. He is their strongest, the most wicked, the most deadly; there is no cure for any one he has struck.

When they are friendly to a man they give him help in his work, putting their strength into his body. Or they may tell him where to find treasure, hidden gold; or through certain wise men or women who have learned from them or can ask and get their knowledge they will tell where cattle that have strayed may be found, or they will cure the sick or tell if a sickness is not to be cured. They will sometimes work as if against their own will or intention, giving back to the life of our world one who had received the call to go over to their own. They call many there, summoning them perhaps through the eye of a neighbour, the evil eye, or by a touch, a blow, a fall, a sudden terror. Those who have received their touch waste away from this world, lending their strength to the invisible ones; for the strength of a human body is needed by the shadows, it may be in their fighting, and certainly in their hurling to win the goal. Young men are taken for this, young mothers are taken that they may give the breast to newly born children among the Sidhe, young girls that they may themselves become mothers there.

While these are away a body in their likeness, or the likeness of a body, is left lying in their place. They may be given leave to return to their village after a while, seven years it may be, or twice or three times seven. But some are sent back only at the end of the years allotted them at the time of their birth, old spent men and women, thought to have been dead a long time, given back to die and be buried on the face of the earth.

The dead are often seen among them, and will give help in danger to comrade or brother or friend. Sometimes they have a penance to work out, and will come and ask the living for help, for prayers, for the payment of a debt. They may wander in some strange shape, or be bound in the one place, or go through the air as birds. When the Sidhe pass by in a blast of wind we should say some words of blessing, for there may be among them some of our own dead. The dead are of the nature of the Saints, mortals who have put on immortality, who have known the troubles of the world. The Sidhe have been, like the Angels, from before the making of the earth. In the old times in Ireland they were called gods or the children of gods; now it is laid down they are those Angels who were cast out of heaven, being proud.

LADY GREGORY, Preface to *Visions and Beliefs*

SPELLS

As a rule it is very little use enquiring about spells. 'There used to be a lot of them in the old days, but the priests put them down.' That particular locality was just then greatly afflicted by a county council doctor whose only method of curing erysipelas was by treating it, which, as everyone knows, is a long and wearisome process compared with the spell. (I have the spell against erysipelas, in case any of my readers cares to try it.) Our host told us how he had seen his own father bleeding to death on the roadway and how the wise woman stopped it with a spell. (I have the spell against bleeding too, but though I have tried it, it has no effect on me.) Many of the spells are common to the whole of Gaelic-speaking Ireland, but others vary from parish to parish. In that particular parish there was a charm which cured certain diseases of cattle, and consisted of some stones sewn up in a bag. No one was ever permitted to know where the bag was at any given time, and whoever needed it had to make a pilgrimage from door to door till he found the family who had it. On the other hand, our hostess, who was from another parish, pointed out that it had no charm against bed-wetting, such as her own parish specialised in.

FRANK O'CONNOR, *Munster, Leinster and Connaught*

CURSING STONES

An old Irish custom, which one hears of, is 'the fire of stones.' A person who wished to curse another, collected a large number of smooth, water-rounded stones and heaped them in the form of a peat-fire. He then knelt in front of the stones and solemnly cursed his victim and invoked ill-luck and misfortune, not only on him, but also on his descendants for many generations to come. The phrase 'until these stones go on fire' was added. Finally, the curser took the stones and hid them singly in inaccessible places with a separate curse on each.

CURSING CONTEST

A rate-collector, named Willis, generally expressed his displeasure at the delay in paying the rate-demands by loudly cursing the tenant. One day he called to a farmer, called Murphy, and found that he did not have the ready cash to meet his obligations. Willis began to curse him but Murphy replied in such a fluent fashion that the competitive soul of Willis was aroused. He promised Murphy that if he defeated him in a cursing-contest he would remit the rates and pay them out of his own pocket. If Willis won on the other hand, Murphy promised that he would raise the money somewhere, no matter how humiliating this admission of poverty was. The two commenced cursing and eventually Willis said:

> May your hens take the disorder (the fowl-pest), your cows the crippen (phosphorosis), and your calves the white scour! May yourself go stone-blind so that you will not know your wife from a hay-stack!

To this sally Murphy retorted in the following manner and defeated his opponent:

> May the seven terriers of hell sit on the spool of your breast and bark in at your soul-case!

In this interesting manner the good farmer Murphy secured a total rebate of his rates for the year.

PATRICK C. PARER, *Book of Irish Curses*

COLOURS OF THE WINDS

They say pigs can see the wind, and that it is red. In very old times the Irish believed that there were twelve different winds with twelve colours.

P. W. JOYCE, *English As We Speak It In Ireland*

Old Mathers was eyeing me.

'What is your colour?' he asked.

'My colour?'

'Surely you know you have a colour?'

'People often remark on my red face.'

'I do not mean that at all.'

I saw it was necessary to question old Mathers carefully.

'Do you refuse to explain this question about the colours?'

'No,' he said. He slapped more tea in his cup.

'No doubt you are aware the winds have colours,' he said. I thought he settled himself more restfully in his chair and changed his face till it looked a little bit benign.

'I never noticed it.'

'A record of this belief will be found in the literature of all ancient peoples. There are four winds and eight sub-winds, each with its own colour. The wind from the east is a deep purple, from the south a fine shining silver. The north wind is a hard black and the west is amber. People in the old days had the power of perceiving these colours and could spend a day sitting quietly on a hillside watching the beauty of the winds, their fall and rise and changing hues, the magic of neighbouring winds when they are inter-weaved like ribbons at a wedding. It was a better occupation than gazing at news-papers. The sub-winds had colours of indescribable delicacy, a reddish-yellow half-way between silver and purple, a greyish-green which was related equally to black and brown. What could be more exquisite than a countryside swept lightly by cool rain reddened by the south-west breeze!'

'Can *you* see these colours?' I asked.

'No.'

'You were asking me what my colour was. How do people get their colours?'

'A person's colour,' he answered slowly, 'is the colour of the wind prevailing at his birth.'

'What is your own colour?'

'Light yellow.'

'And what is the point of knowing your colour or having a colour at all?'

'For one thing you can tell the length of your life from it. Yellow means a long life and the lighter the better.'

'Please explain.'

'It is a question of making little gowns,' he said informatively.

'Little gowns?'

'Yes. When I was born there was a certain policeman present who had the gift of wind-watching. The gift is getting very rare these days. Just after I was born he went outside and examined the colour of the wind that was blowing across the hill. He had a secret bag with him full of certain materials and bottles and he had tailor's instruments also. He was outside for about ten minutes. When he came in again he had a little gown in his hand and he made my mother put it on me.'

'Where did he get this gown?' I asked in surprise.

'He made it himself secretly in the backyard, very likely in the cowhouse. It was very thin and slight like the very finest of spider's muslin. You would not see it at all if you held it against the sky but at certain angles of the light you might at times accidentally notice the edge of it. It was the purest and most perfect manifestation of the outside skin of light yellow. This yellow was the colour of my birth-wind.'

'I see,' I said.

'Every time my birthday came,' old Mathers said, 'I was presented with another little gown of the same identical quality except that it was put on over the other one and not in place of it. You may appreciate the extreme delicacy and fineness of the material when I tell you that even at five years old with five of these gowns together on me, I still appeared to be naked. It was, however, an unusual yellowish sort of nakedness. Of course there was no objection to wearing other clothes over the gown. I usually wore an overcoat. But every year I got a new gown.'

'Where did you get them?' I asked.

'From the police. They were brought to my own home until I was big enough to call to the barracks for them.'

'And how does all this enable you to predict your span of life?'

'I will tell you. No matter what your colour is, it will be represented faithfully in your birth-gown. With each year and each gown, the colour will get deeper and more pronounced. In my own case I had attained a bright full-blown yellow at fifteen although the colour was so light at birth as to be imperceptible. I am now nearing seventy and the colour is a light brown. As my gowns come to me through the years ahead, the colour will deepen to dark brown, then a dull mahogany and from that ultimately to that very dark sort of brownness one associates usually with stout.'

'Yes?'

'In a word the colour gradually deepens gown by gown and year by year until it appears to be black. Finally a day will come when the addition of one further gown will actually achieve real and full blackness. On that day I will die.'

FLANN O'BRIEN, *The Third Policeman*

GOD'S WORD

THE GOD IN THE TREE

This was eleven years ago, at Gallarus Oratory, on the Dingle
Peninsula, in Co. Kerry, an early Christian, dry-stone oratory,
about the size of a large turf-stack. Inside, in the dark of the
stone, it feels as if you are sustaining a great pressure, bowing
under like the generations of monks who must have bowed
down in meditation and reparation on that floor. I felt the
weight of Christianity in all its rebuking aspects, its calls to
self-denial and self-abnegation, its humbling of the proud flesh
and insolent spirit. But coming out of the cold heart of the
stone, into the sunlight and the dazzle of grass and sea, I felt
a lift in my heart, a surge towards happiness that must have
been experienced over and over again by those monks as they
crossed that same threshold centuries ago.

SEAMUS HEANEY, *Preoccupations*

THE HERMIT

Grant me sweet Christ the grace to find –
Son of the living God –
A small hut in a lonesome spot
To make it my abode

A little pool but very clear
To stand beside the place
Where all men's sins are washed away
By sanctifying grace.

A pleasant woodland all about
To shield it from the wind
And make a home for singing birds
Before it and behind.

A lovely Church, a home for God
Bedecked with linen fine
Where over the white gospel page
The Gospel candles shine

My share of clothing and of food
From the King of fairest face
And I to sit at times alone
And pray in every place.

THE PILGRIM

In timgér celebrad cóir
    d'innsi móir macc Míled múaid?
Indom tairber fo Chríst cuing
    ria techt tar tuinn Mara Ruaid?

In ráidiubsa, rád ndíuit ndían,
    mo choibsen cían, comol crúaid?
In ferfat, a Rí na néll,
    frassa mo dér tar mo grúaid?

In tiurr mo láim do cach crécht
    for brú tuinne tinnbi bárc?
In fuicéb oc mara múr
    slicht mo da glún isin trácht?

In toicéb mo churchán cíar
    ós oicén uchtlethan án?
In reg, a Rí ríchid réil
    as mo thoil féin for in sál?

Imba sessach, imba seng,
    imba tressach tuirme glonn
a Chríst, in cuingéna frimm,
    ó thí co techt tar linn lonn?

Shall I go, O King of the Mysteries, after my fill of cushions and music, to turn my face on the shore and my back on my native land?
Shall I be in poverty in the battle through the grace of the King, a King who does not fail, without great honour or a famous chariot, without silver and without a horse?
Without heady drink that intoxicates a throng, without a stout

tribe, without retainers to protect me, without a swift shield or any
weapon, without cup, ale, or drinking-horn?

Without soft clothes that are pleasant to look at, without cushions,
which are no friend of any saint, but beech-twigs of virtue under a
hard quilt for my body?

Shall I say a long farewell to the great island of the sons of proud
Míl? Shall I offer myself under Christ's yoke before I cross the waters
of the Red Sea?

Shall I make my long confession, swiftly and simply, on this hard
occasion? Shall I, O King of the Clouds, shed showers of tears over
my cheek?

Shall I cut my hand with every sort of wound on the breast of the
wave which wrecks boats? Shall I leave the track of my two knees
on the strand by the shore?

Shall I take my little black curragh over the broad-breasted, glori-
ous ocean? O King of the bright kingdom, shall I go of my own choice
upon the sea?

Whether I be strong or poor, or mettlesome so as to be recounted
in tales, O Christ, will you help me when it comes to going upon the
wild sea?

FRANK O'CONNOR, *A Golden Treasury of Irish Poetry*
AD 600–1200

HOLY WELLS

At a little distance there is to be found one of those holy wells
round which the inhabitants perform their devotions. This well
is very famous, and the people come from afar. They pretend
or assert that it can cure all evils, and the devotion consists in
going round the well, bare-footed, seven times while reciting
prayers, kneeling for a moment at each turn before a black
stone, which seems to have been a tombstone, and, while
kneeling, they rub the hand over three heads which are cut
in the stone, and which are much worn by reason of this
hand-rubbing and kissing. Afterwards they pass the hand
which has touched the stone over the part of the body which
is afflicted, drink a large glass of the water, and wash their feet
in the current. Children are sometimes plunged seven times
into the cold water, and I have seen people, well clad and

having the appearance of being in comfortable circumstances, perform these ceremonies just like the others. I have also seen a very pretty young girl kissing these ugly stones, and I could not help thinking that I would have been a much better restorer if she had paid the reverence to me.

This well is widely renowned in the country, and even the Protestants, who are not very numerous here, when they have tried other remedies in vain, will make up their minds to try the well and go through the usual performances like their Catholic friends. The greater part of these peasants, however, come in a rather careless spirit, seemingly more with a desire to meet their friends than to perform penitences. Speaking to one of the visitors I asked him what was the benefit to be derived from this water. His reply was that he could not tell, and when I asked him why he went through the usual performances, all he could say was 'to do what the others do and to see the women.' In effect, it is at these wells that a great number of marriages are arranged. It is in vain that the priest of the parish has often forbidden his people to go to such places; they have followed this custom so long before the establishment of Christianity that they cannot be broken off it.

DE LATOCHAYE, *A Frenchman's Walk Through Ireland*

TIGHT WITHIN HIS GRASP

All this week however I have not felt well. Have been without appetite and pursued by attacks of nausea. What is it, if not just Ireland? . . . At Mass the church here is so crowded that one cannot worship. Irish Catholicism is like a vice, crushing the congregation like nuts. The Irish God is not loving. He is a tyrant. The people are tight within his grasp. Unlike Latins they are subdued by their Church, not elevated by it. They derive from it no inspiration, recreation or romance. Here it is grey and puritanical. In the church the men herd on the Epistle side, the women on the Gospel side like battery hens. One senses that their appalling mendacity and untrustworthiness are the consequence of their age-long abortive attempts to escape the clutch of the priests.

JAMES LEES MILNE, *Midway on the Waves*

186

Our mother seldom had time to go for a leisurely walk: she was too busy, or too tired after strenuous work, or she had to go 'just there and back' when she visited sick people, so that when one day she asked me if I should like to go for a walk with her I was astonished and delighted.

'Is anyone ill?' I asked her, 'is Mary Deasy worse?'

'I haven't heard,' said my mother, 'but we will take her some cough mixture as we go by. I thought you and I might go down to the lake.'

This was so unusual that I felt half afraid I might have done something for which I deserved a lecture, but mother's face re-assured me.

The Deasy children were playing in the dust of the path outside the cabin; all except Timmy, the eldest of the six, who was minding his mother in the bedroom where they all slept at night. The cabin had only two rooms, a kitchen and a bedroom, small and stuffy, with panes of thick glass built into the wall to let in a little light. A hen dashed out, cackling, as we entered, leaving an egg behind her on the hearth.

'Must I go in?' I whispered, hanging back.

Mother nodded and we went into the inner room where Mary Deasy was propped up in bed by a bundle of sacks surmounted by a dingy pillow. She was flushed and exhausted by a bout of coughing, but smiled gallantly. Mother gave her a dose of the carrigeen mixture and talked quietly while the sick woman recovered her breath.

'I d'know will I get it done in time,' she said, patting the white linen which she had been sewing, 'I've another yard and more to seam up before it'll be done. I d'know can I hold out so long?'

'If you will lend me your thimble, I will sew some of it,' mother said.

Mary was unwilling. ' 'Tis like your kindness, ma'am,' she said, 'but I'm wishful to set the last stitch in it meself if so be I can. I'm thinkin' 'tis havin' the sewin' that keeps me here for another day – or mebbe two – with himself and the childer, God help them!' She smiled again. 'Ye'll give an eye to them, I know, ma'am, till himself gets married to me cousin, Nancy

Sheehan. If ye could take Timmy on the farm I'd know he'd get plenty to eat.'

My mother signed to me to go out; my knees were knocking together and I felt faint. Timmy, in the kitchen, stared at me.

'Could ye beat up the egg while I heat a drop o'milk?' he asked me, and I responded as best I could.

From the inner room I heard my mother's voice, gentle, re-assuring, and the low, continuous coughing of the sick woman.

'Me mammy's been anointed,' Timmy told me confidentially. 'Father Ryan was here last night. He told me father she wouldn't last the week out. 'Tis a grand place where she's goin'; 'tis the other side of the world anyway, an' she'll thravel there in a box . . . Mammy said not to mind about that and about her looking quare, because she'll be enjoyin' herself when she gets there – 'twill be better than a fair! But . . . it's lonesome I'll be for her . . . and I d'know will I be able to mind the childer and them so bold.'

Mother was saying, 'Good-bye, my dear; God be on the road with you.'

Mary answered very cheerfully, 'And with you, ma'am! Me blessin' on you for scatterin' me fears. *Timmy! Timmy!* Let you have a look for me thimble under the bed. I'll get on wid me sewin' before 'tis dark.'

It was her shroud that she was making.

MARY CARBERRY, *The Farm by Lough Gur*

THE KEEN

After Mass this morning an old woman was buried. She lived in the cottage next mine, and more than once before noon I heard a faint echo of the keen. I did not go to the wake for fear my presence might jar upon the mourners, but all last evening I could hear the strokes of a hammer in the yard, where, in the middle of a little crowd of idlers, the next of kin laboured slowly at the coffin. To-day, before the hour for the funeral, poteen was served to a number of men who stood about upon the road, and a portion was brought to me in my room. Then the coffin was carried out sewn loosely in sailcloth, and held near the ground by three cross-poles lashed upon the top. As we moved down to the low eastern portion of the island, nearly all the men, and all the oldest women, wearing petticoats over their hands, came out and joined in the procession.

While the grave was being opened the women sat down among the flat tombstones, bordered with a pale fringe of early bracken, and began the wild keen, or crying for the dead. Each old woman, as she took her turn in the leading recitative, seemed possessed for the moment with a profound ecstasy of grief, swaying to and fro, and bending her forehead to the stone before her, while she called out to the dead with a perpetually recurring chant of sobs.

All round the graveyard other wrinkled women, looking out from under the deep red petticoats that cloaked them, rocked themselves with the same rhythm, and intoned the inarticulate chant that is sustained by all as an accompaniment.

The morning had been beautifully fine, but as they lowered the coffin into the grave, thunder rumbled overhead and hailstones hissed among the bracken.

In Inishmaan one is forced to believe in a sympathy between man and nature, and at this moment when the thunder sounded a death-peal of extraordinary grandeur above the voices of the women, I could see the faces near me stiff and drawn with emotion.

This grief of the keen is no personal complaint for the death of one woman over eighty years, but seems to contain the whole passionate rage that lurks somewhere in every native of the island. In this cry of pain the inner consciousness of the people seems to lay itself bare for an instant, and to reveal the mood of beings who feel their isolation in the face of a universe that wars on them with winds and seas. They are usually silent, but in the presence of death all outward show of indifference or patience is forgotten, and they shriek with pitiable despair before the horror of the fate to which they all are doomed.

Before they covered the coffin an old man kneeled down by the grave and repeated a simple prayer for the dead.

There was an irony in these words of atonement and

Catholic belief spoken by voices that were still hoarse with the cries of pagan desperation.

A little beyond the grave I saw a line of old women who had recited in the keen sitting in the shadow of a wall beside the roofless shell of the church. They were still sobbing and shaken with grief, yet they were beginning to talk again of the daily trifles that veil from them the terror of the world.

J. M. SYNGE, *The Aran Islands*

WHO CAME HAVE GONE

Who have come have gone, who shall come must
    go,
But the graces of God shall forever flow.
DOUGLAS HYDE, *Studies and Translations from the Irish*

TO THE HOLY TRINITY

Three folds in cloth, yet there is but the one cloth.
Three joints in a finger, yet there is but the one finger.
Three leaves in a shamrock, yet there is but the one
    shamrock.
Frost, snow and ice . . . yet the three are only water.
Three Persons in God likewise, and but the one God.
THOMAS KINSELLA, *Poems of the Dispossessed*

Like my father and mother I had only one escape: humbly to accept the Will of God. It is the escape from bitterness that we Irish have taken for centuries, and it has not worked out too badly, insofar as we have come through all sorts of oppressions and misfortunes a cheerful, good-humoured, loyal, hardworking, tenacious people. The Will of God prevailed for a long time with me. I went through most of my boyhood unquestioning Heaven. What broke it apart, in the end, was pity and anger: the first for my mother, whom I loved so dearly that I could not bear the sight of her unhappiness; and the second, far later, for my people, in a bitter rage that they should be obliged to endure so much.

SEAN O'FAOLAIN, *Vive Moi*

INTERVIEW WITH THE PARISH PRIEST AT TUAM

You have seen, Sir, how I am looked upon in this village. The people love me, Sir, and they have reason to love me, for I myself love them. They have confidence in me, and I in them. Every man considers me in some way as one of his brothers, the eldest in the family. How does this happen, Sir? It is that the people and I every day have need of each other. The people share liberally with me the fruit of their labours, and I give them my time, my care, my whole soul. I am nothing without them, and without me they would succumb under the weight of their sorrows. Between us there is a ceaseless exchange of affectionate feelings.

ALEXIS DE LA TOCQUEVILLE, *Journey in Ireland*

I'm a small-town Irish Protestant, a 'lace-curtain' Protestant. Poor Protestants in Ireland are a sliver of people caught between the past – Georgian Ireland with its great houses and all the rest of it – and the new, bustling, Catholic state. Without knowing any of this, without its ever occurring to me, I was able to see things a little more clearly than I would have if I had belonged to either of those worlds.

. . .

I don't really think of myself as religious . . . I only ever go to church in Ireland. I don't like the Church of England. I feel much more drawn towards Catholicism when I'm in England – not that I'd do anything about it. I always feel that Protestantism in England is strangely connected with the military. All the cathedrals here are full of military honours. It's part of an establishment with the armed forces; tombs, rolls of honour, that sort of thing. It's a strange combination. The Protestant Church of Ireland is a shrunken, withered little church that I'm quite attracted by.

WILLIAM TREVOR, *The Art of Fiction, Paris Review No.110*

Mission stalls did their best trade in holy pictures. There were two sizes, prayerbook and wall. St Joseph was easily the most popular subject. Usually he was depicted looking out over the viewer's shoulder (as though standing on a wall), a lily in his right hand. St Antony of Padua was popular too. He was one of the handiest of the saints: if you lost something and prayed to him, he'd find it for you. Youth had its own saints: Dominic Savio and Maria Goretti, both notorious for their purity.

Then there were statues. In this branch of business Our Lady led the field. Easy for her, of course, since she appeared in so many different liveries. Our Lady of Lourdes, of Guadeloupe, of Mount Carmel . . . Runner-up in statue-sales was, surprisingly, Blessed Martin de Pores, the first Latin American to be beatified. The lesson of his status was, presumably, that there was hope for everyone – hence his popularity. Lastly there were the treasures, the rosaries that had crucifixes with relics in them, the miraculous medals, the white prayerbooks with ornate, gold-looking locks attached to their sides which were considered ideal for little girls.

It says something for the mood generated by the Mission that nobody showed any curiosity about the stallholders. Only now does it occur to me to wonder who they were and where they came from and how they knew where to come. Perhaps the various preaching orders issued a calendar of Missions according to which the pedlars planned itineraries. Maybe these camp-followers were members of some lay order, their plaster figures and oleographic images a subtle descent to the vivid inarticulacy of the faithful's creed, against which the power of the preacher (his licence to speak) could be measured to his advantage. Or could the portable store have been a penance – all that packing and unpacking – imposed by some vindictively imaginative confessor?

We invariably had Redemptorists for our Mission. Our own clergy, who hired them, wouldn't have any others. They were right, no doubt: Jesuits would have talked over our heads, and certainly wouldn't have roared enough at us, and probably were in any case much too expensive.

GEORGE O'BRIEN, *The Village of Longing*

PENAL DAYS

Of course, the Catholic Plunketts suffered for their religion. One of the possessions of the house was a chest of drawers, which appears as much as possible like such a piece of furniture as you would find in a servant's room. It was of the plainest wood and had china handles to it. The top lifted up and revealed inside an altar perfectly arranged for saying Mass. It was a relic of the Penal Days, when Mass might only be said secretly at Killeen as elsewhere, with scouts posted to watch for any danger. A hurried warning and the lid could be closed down, the priest hidden, the congregation scattered.

LADY FINGALL, *Memoirs*

DEATH

30th . . . My wife very ill. May Almighty God cure her. My poor children will suffer a great loss if she dies suddenly. *One's end is sleep, and a woman wakes her own corpse.* She sleeps badly. Her leg is paining her. She is failing greatly. She stayed up two or three nights a week ago, and that left her very weak. She has a bad cough. God help her . . .

A troup of actors were performing on the Fair Green. They danced, played music and performed acrobatics. A cloudy night.

July 1st . . . Raining all the morning from day-break until ten o'clock. A calm north eastern wind. Dry at mid-day. Showery at the close of day, with a lively cold north-west wind.

Now, at this moment, at eleven o'clock at night my wife died, having received Extreme Unction, by the will of God.

2nd . . . A fine thin-clouded sunny day. A mild west wind. I was never alone until this day.

The Diary of Humphrey O'Sullivan, (1827) (Trans. Thomas de Bhaldraith)

'Everyone in the town knew that I was the seventh son of a seventh son, and that can be very tough. People were always expecting great things from you, and my mother used to hide me away in the room when anyone called at the door. A pain in the back and a pain here, and at the time I was only four or five years of age.

I don't know how we managed and that was something of a miracle itself, for we were very poor, and my father had a very small wage. The seventh son has always been looked on as something different, and even somewhere like India he turns out to be a Guru . . . someone blessed or something. You feel different from other people. At school you are going to be considered a freak, so that means you have to do far more than others to be normal.

The strange thing is that I never had a child's mind. I could pick up the papers at three years old and read out to my father. And then I had a queer sort of birth. First of all I was born by breech . . . and I came feet first. Then I was born with a caul, which is a thing around your face, and then to be the seventh son of the seventh. Then my grandfather was a healer and my aunt a herbalist. I had two uncles who were herbalists and my grandmother was a fortune teller. In the name of God I had it every way.

From when I was a small boy I was automatically a doctor, and they would be saying to me, Dr Carroll do this, and Dr Carroll do that. They would come up to me in some sort of pain and say, 'Holy God, what disease have I?' And this can be very tough because they are expecting great things. 'Why don't you go to hospitals?' some people used to say. 'There are sick people there, and you can do a lot of cures.' Surely to God if I were to go to hospital and put myself on people and say 'I'll cure you', then I am becoming God. It has to be a request to do the thing . . . they have to need help. And there's not one person who comes to the door, but that they do need help.

And the other thing you must have is a sense of humour. Because you can mix a very serious thing with a good sense of humour. For who wants a person with a long face coming to the door with someone dying? Other healers have secretaries taking money from you, and what are they giving you? Charging a fee for something that has been given free. In all the thirty-five years that I have been doing it I have never charged a fee. It was always up to the person, what they gave. You can't buy health.

People get sick for all sorts of reasons. Of course cancer is more prevalent. Look at the food and the fertilizer that goes on everything. All you have to do is to take the tinned peas and when you open them, what do they do but turn black. There's an acid in the tin, but that goes down into your stomach and it's all poison.

Another reason why people are sick is because we are suffering from older generations of people. Those who wished harm on someone, those who went around putting eggs into hay and wishing envy. For instance, how many times did the priest get into the pulpit in the old days and curse some individual from the altar? If we are human we cannot all be saints, and something will upset us. 'Oh God I could kill them' you might say; but you see, the curse of people is put on others, and it's on the children, and they suffer for the guilty. So illness does come from the older generation, and Christ has nothing to do with it.

When I was young the person who had the greatest influence on my life was Padre Pio. I got a relic from him when I was thirteen, and from then on I fell in love with him. I would say it was love, but not the sort of love you feel for a woman, but a burning thing that consumes you, and I have never felt the same for anyone. I visited him once, and at that time there was no sort of commercialism like £5 for a Mass and £5 for relics, and everything was very simple. I stayed with him in a room for more than an hour with an interpreter, and his words to me were 'You are born with a gift that God has given you, and use it for the suffering souls, and never think of yourself above another person or being special.'

I have been very lucky with priests and with doctors and the medical profession. I have been recommended by the medical profession and by the clergy. I don't infringe on the religion, I don't go around with a candle in my hand. I don't get you to say prayers and give you penance, I don't give you medicines or herbs, and another thing I don't go round drowning you with holy water on a frosty day.

PETER SOMERVILLE-LARGE, *Cappaghglass*

Melleray stands alone on the mountain tract surrounded by the gardens, orchards and pasture lands won from the coarse surrounding moors. The main building, of cut stone, is forbidding in its bareness. Of its completion over a century ago, a booklet on the history of Mount Melleray says, 'As for definite architectural style of any kind, the brethren were too much intent on economy and haste to concern themselves about that. In fact, except for its lancet windows and the small square Gothic church tower, the buildings can scarcely be said to have any special architectural form.' Small wonder when 'there was no quarry to furnish stones; the material was sought and found in the land under preparation for tillage, not in any one place, but here and there over the entire area. There was no lime, no sand.'

But the look of coldness comes from improvements made in 1950; 'The ancient Gothic windows were to be removed and in their place a double row of steel-framed windows were to be put in,' resulting in 'more perfect ventilation, better lighting and greater security from the severe cold of the winter season.' In a lower, warmer building to its side, a gift shop was tended by two brothers and next to it a door opened into the wide hall of the visitors' building. A tour of the monastery would begin in a few minutes. Women could not go. I felt a familiar pang, a mixture of panic and sadness, at being excluded for being a woman. It must be the underlying tone of a Negro's whole life.

The pang dismissed by the director of human relationships in my head, I said good-bye to P as he disappeared into the sacred territory with a small band of men and boys.

A dirt road followed the high walls of the gardens to the north of the buildings. At the far end, through openings of gates and apertures, glimpses could be had of the stalls for milk cows, stables for workhorses, and in one I looked into a greenhouse of staked tomato plants. Beyond, through its glass walls I could see neat rows of lettuce and cabbage. Fruit trees growing above the wall cast shadows on the end rows.

Across the road were the chicken houses and pens for roosters. A narrow path passed them going up the bare mountain, on top of which a great cross made its plea to the sky. A monk was coming down the path. His hands were folded into the sleeves of his garment and strings held up the hem of his white habit revealing thick stockings and sturdy shoes. Hesitant to invade his privacy, nevertheless I wanted a look; angling sneaky glances into his cowl, I beheld a face so holy (that is, whole, the etymology being the same), that the fragments of my person could not enter to invade. He opened a gate in the high gray wall and disappeared into the gardens. The pieces of myself probe for information on where, and how, to rejoin. The wholeness of the monk moves in the felt certitude of his maturing.

DEBORAH LOVE, *Annagh Keen*

THE PLEASURE GROUNDS

THE PLEASURE GROUND

Once, when I was a child, and playing in a pleasure ground, I swallowed a poison berry. It fell into my open mouth as I watched my sister climbing among the prickly leaves of a tall Irish yew. Cure, I thought, was impossible: a pain would start, and I should soon and surely die. A terror like the one I now felt had been with me in Ceylon, in the compound with its drains full of deadly snakes. But here we were in the green and snakeless island of Ireland, where you could safely sleep without mosquito nets, and yet this foolishly had happened. It could only be a matter of minutes or perhaps hours. Prayers might prolong the time I had left for living, but as sure as anything the poison had got into my system.

I was about twelve then, and we lived with my mother at my grandfather's house in the west of Ireland, while my father worked for us abroad. Our branch of the family occupied the east wing of the house, which had once been the servants' quarters, not so many years ago when the wage on the land was sixpence a day, and no cure had been found for TB, typhus, or famine fever: dreadful diseases I had managed so far to escape, only to succumb to poison; and of all places, in what was called the pleasure ground.

We were proud of our pleasure ground: we thought it was the oldest and most beautiful in Ireland. It once had a lovers' walk marked out by cedars of Lebanon and Florence Court yews in methodical pairs, with lawns and copper beeches in the centre. The whole garden was surrounded by an Anglo-Irish wall, a great wall of pride and oppression, liberally overgrown with romantic ivy. For years the place had been neglected. Many things had improved in Ireland, but this garden of the ascendancy had declined like the family fortune. A laurel forest now covered the lawn except for a patch kept trimmed by rabbits round the trunk of the beech tree. The yew hedge, where the daughters of high sheriffs had decorously flirted, was now a dark row of trees, and the walks were impassable with briars. My mother devoted herself to restoring this pleasure ground. It had been in her family since the victories of King William of Orange, and the first thing she did was to knock down a huge stretch of the wall which had formerly imprisoned the servants, so that our house lay open to the garden. It was looking on to this pleasure ground, or sitting in the shade of the copper beech, that we did our lessons.

First an hour anxiously passed, and then a day: I had not sickened or died, and the menace of the yew-berry passed. It was the happiest time of my life. We could not be sent to schools abroad because the war was on, and travelling was then impossible. But instead of work being a difficulty, it had here become a delight. Things my mother liked were easy to learn in order to please her; things she disapproved of we grasped in a flash of revolt. One day, struggling through the tall weeds in an orchard just outside the pleasure ground, I came across a very old fig-tree, and searching under its big green leaves I found a number of small hard unripe figs. After this, the fig-tree was mine, and all through that summer I waited for the fruit to ripen; I dug the roots, manured and watered the ground, cut the weeds, sowed seeds of flowers nearby, even a row of carrots: and it was all effortless joy. Eventually I remember eating the fruit, with no fear of poison this time, though as luck would have it I was chased away by some angry wild bees at that very moment.

My mother wanted me to be a diplomat, but the lessons I learnt in that garden were not the right training for a Civil Service career. We were much too wild. Our life went from one extreme to another, from discipline to anarchy. My brother, for instance, had to pass his School Certificate. He also kept a herd of goats in the woods, and one of the kids used to lie under the piano my mother played at our morning prayers.

In the west wing lived our grandparents, in rooms grimy with portraits, especially an ugly one of Cromwell. There was a smell of tow and gun-oil and empty cartridge shells in my grandfather's study, with its racks of shot-guns he taught me to use on rabbits. There was also a Turkish rifle he had picked up on the beach at Gallipoli. Battle-axes hung on hooks, and the stairs were decorated with prints of the fighting in Rangoon, with sepoys in the act of being shot or disembowelled. Black labrador dogs jumped up on you in the pitch-dark flagged and slippery corridors. A portable harmonium waited for Sundays in the hall under the water-glass which told the weather. My grandfather was a clergyman.

It was here in the west wing that I had been born, and my grandmother was always our ally in trouble, sickness, or romance. Here my sister was promised her future husband at cards; here ghosts were real because my grandmother frequently saw them; here were secret chambers she helped us to find – we *did* find one full of rotten muskets – and horrible practical jokes. She was fond of dogs, and I made wreaths to put on their graves at the top of the yew-walk. Moss roses grew by her well: she told me they helped a person to fall in love, and I sniffed them for hours. In her glasshouse she kept my orange tree alive.

My grandmother had been brought up on the far side of the Connemara mountains, on the harsh Atlantic coast. This was fifty miles away, and we used to motor there, from the pleasure ground, on birthdays and other family occasions. My sister used to bring her painting things, and seen through my mother's and my grandmother's eyes, this land which we entered, so stark, wild and simple, was more beautiful than the deeply nurtured garden we had left.

It was a desperately poor part of the country. Huddled among boulders were those whose ancestors had lost the pitiless struggle for the land which ours had won. The planters of our pleasure ground had acquired an estate of 70,000 acres, which famine, revolution, and liberalism had cut down to its present size of 300 acres. But these people lived on five- or only two-and-a-half acre holdings, and we loved them better than our own relations, or the children at the rectory parties we had to attend. They were truly Irish, and that is what my brother and I wanted to be. They seemed sharper, freer, more cunning than we were. Stones, salmon-falls, rain-clouds and drownings had entered and shaped their minds, loaded with ancestral bias. They seemed most mysterious and imaginative to us. Their manners had a real charm instead of a false one, and their singing voices used tones that rasped excitingly against the hymn-tune harmonies we were used to. We wished we could talk like them. Old people among them had all the time in the world to tell us fantastic stories. It was the antidote which the poisoning in the pleasure ground needed.

Twice before, much earlier in my life, as far back as I can remember, we had lived in the Connemara hills, first by a lake and later by the sea, that greatest of all pleasure grounds. The house by the lake had a garden with a deep well which I fell into while playing with my brother. This left no mark of fear, but gave me a love and a respect for water. Near the lake was a grey Norman castle with a black stream running by the walls, and sloe hedges beside the lanes, where we walked with our pails of milk and picked wild strawberries. Even then I was terrified I might have swallowed the wrong berry.

The pleasure ground period did not last for ever. Thanks to winning a scholarship, I was sent off to boarding school in England. Death and emigration soon left my grandmother alone in the place, and the garden fell back into anarchy and decay. Chickens scratched on my mother's lupin-beds; hay was scythed on the tennis court; the laurels and the rabbits increased; the beech tree was cut down and sold for firewood; cows strayed through the rusty gates, munched yew-leaves, and died within the hour (they *were* poisonous!). Now my grandmother was mistress of a beautiful disorder, living on the last trees of a once great forest. The yew still bore a crop of berries, the fig-tree had survived; but the discipline of the garden had died. The spirit that I was looking for in the yew-berry, the fig, and the beech tree had withdrawn – that spirit which had once made poetry and music and painting, even mathematics, an effortless delight. There was no masculine energy in the place, to mend walls, plant new trees, sow and cultivate and labour, and I felt lost, and guilty.

So I went back to that older, earlier pleasure ground in the treeless hills, on the sea's edge, and rediscovered Connemara. There at the age of nineteen I abandoned myself to mountains, lakes, and waterfalls; I rolled naked in snow, and stretched without clothes on the cold ground on summer nights. I wanted to write poetry, and believed that some day, like the ripening of the figs, I should taste that fruit and it would not be poison, nor would the bees chase me from the tree. I did not dream that it would take so long and be so difficult to produce a first crop. As I grew older the garden grew wilder, losing its form as trees were felled, and its spirit as the old people died and the young left the country; so I searched more and more into the origins of that garden till I found them finally in the sea.

Effort and discipline, paths, spades, bill-hooks, walls and gates are all needed to keep a garden, which has to be cultivated, and not just reaped as in the act of fishing. Our own hands have to give the garden shape and structure. Poems are quite unlike the sea; they are like gardens in their making, in that our task is to give shape to whatever grows: to use words to control that force that shakes the berries from the branch, that throws up one fisherman drowned on the shore and another saved, that drops a poison seed into the ground.

RICHARD MURPHY, from An Irish Childhood,
ed. A. Norman Jeffares and Antony Kamm

My Mother was a famous Œconomist, as she was factotum to my Grandmother Lady Desart (since dead) but my father was far from being a careful Providore – however when she arrived at Carrick, she found her New Abode most conveniently furnished – but in a Week, or fortnight, one Neighbour sent for his Chairs, another for his Tables, and so forth, till nothing remaind but the bare Walls – My Father and his friends laughd at her Embarassment, and furnishing the House anew, with other Expences, kept them under Water for a long time, but her Cleverness overcame all Obstacles, and they were at length comfortably settled in their beautiful little villa near Carrick on Suir –

DOROTHEA HERBERT, Retrospections (1739–70)

BOWEN'S COURT

Our post town, Kildorrery, on the top of its hill, lies about a mile east of the Lower, or Farahy, gates. The Farahy glebe lands, with the church and rectory, are carved out of the demesne. In no other direction lies any town or larger village, except Shanballymore, for seven or eight miles. Mallow is thirteen, Fermoy twelve, Mitchelstown eight and Doneraile seven miles from Bowen's Court. Inside and about the house and in the demesne woods you feel transfixed by the surrounding emptiness; it gives depth to the silence, quality to the light. The land round Bowen's Court, even under its windows, has an unhumanized air the house does nothing to change. Here are, even, no natural features, view or valley, to which the house may be felt to relate itself. It has set, simply, its pattern of trees and avenues on the virgin, anonymous countryside. Like Flaubert's ideal book about nothing, its sustains itself on itself by the inner force of its style.

Bowen's Court, finished in 1776, is a high bare Italianate house. It was intended to form a complete square, but the north-east corner is missing. Indoors, the plan is simple; the rooms are large, lofty and few. The house stands three stories high, with, below, a basement sunk in an area. Outside the front door a terrace, supported on an unseen arch, bridges the area: from this terrace the steps descend to the gravel sweep. The house is built of limestone from a nearby quarry; the south front and long west side are faced with cut stone – the mouldings and corners are marble-sharp. The east side and north back are more roughly finished – the rest of the cut stone was kept for the stables' front. Inside the angle where the north-east corner is missing, ghostly outlines of what should have been doors appear – in the builder's view the house was still incomplete.

Bowen's Court shows almost living changes of colour. In fine weather the limestone takes on a warm whitish powdery bloom – with its parapet cut out against a bright blue sky this might almost be a building in Italy. After persistent rain the stone stains a dark slate and comes out in irregular black streaks – till the house blots into its dark rainy background of trees. In cold or warm dusks it goes either steel or lavender; in full moonlight it glitters like silvered chalk.

The great bare block – not a creeper touches it – is broken regularly by windows: in the south façade there are twenty (the hall door takes the place of one of them), in the west side eighteen, in the shorter east side six, in the north back six – and I exlude from this count all the basement windows which, heavily barred look into the area. In the south façade the windows have mouldings, on the other sides they are set in plain. All this expanse of glass, with its different reflections, does much to give Bowen's Court character. When the sun is low, in the early mornings or evenings, the house seems, from the outside, to be riddled with light.

Indoors, the rooms with these big windows not only reflect the changes of weather but seem to contain the weather itself.

The high Venetian window on the staircase, looking north to the mountains through a plantation of spruce, sends in, if never direct sunshine, sun-colours that are almost as bright – this is most of all so in winter. And on winter mornings, when the late-rising sun throws the shadows of the circle of elms in a fan down the frosty lawn in front of the house until their tip touches the steps, the plaster and marble indoors, even the white woodwork, looks also frosty and hard. When rain moves in vague grey curtains across the country, or stands in a sounding pillar over the roof and trees, grey quivers steadily on the indoor air, giving the rooms, whichever room you go into, the resigned look of being exposed to rain. The metal of autumn sharpens and burnishes everything in the house. And summer's drone and spring's yellow-green rustle penetrate everywhere. The front and corner rooms get so much sun, when there *is* sun, that mahogany doors and tables bleach to a pale tan. On summer afternoons the rooms at the south-west corner become as dazzling as lakes.

ELIZABETH BOWEN, *Bowen's Court*

LISMORE CASTLE

She also persists in its being very damp. It certainly feels so, though I know not why: for though close to the water it is on a rock. Hart and Caroline had many disputes on the damp, when last night she suddenly opened the door very wide, saying, 'Pray walk in, sir. I have no doubt you are the lawful possessor, and my cousin only an interloper, usurping your usual habitation.' For a long time nothing came, when at last, with great solemnity and many pauses, in hopped a toad, Caroline following with two candles, to treat the master of the castle with proper respect, she said.

Letter from Lady Bessborough to Lord Granville
describing Caroline Lamb recuperating from her love
affair with Byron (1812)

DIRECTIONS TO THE WAITING MAID

If you are in a great family, and my lady's woman, my lord may probably like you, although you are not half so handsome as his own lady. In this case, take care to get as much out of him as you can; and never allow him the smallest liberty, not the squeezing of your hand, unless he puts a guinea into it; so by degrees make him pay accordingly for every new attempt, doubling upon him in proportion to the concessions you allow, and always struggling, and threatening to cry out, or tell your lady, although you receive his money: five guineas for handling your breasts is a cheap pennyworth, although you seem to resist with all your might; but never allow him the last favour under a hundred guineas, or a settlement of twenty pounds a year for life.

JONATHAN SWIFT, *Servants in General*

A LANDLORD'S GARDEN IN COUNTY WICKLOW

Everyone is used in Ireland to the tragedy that is bound up with the lives of farmers and fishing people; but in this garden one seemed to feel the tragedy of the landlord class also, and of the innumerable old families that are quickly dwindling away. These owners of the land are not much pitied at the present day, or much deserving of pity; and yet one cannot quite forget that they are the descendants of what was at one time, in the eighteenth century, a high-spirited and highly-cultivated aristocracy. The broken greenhouses and mouse-eaten libraries, that were designed and collected by men who voted with Grattan, are perhaps as mournful in the end as the four mud walls that are so often left in Wicklow as the only remnants of a farmhouse. The desolation of this life is often of a peculiarly local kind, and if a playwright chose to go through the Irish country houses he would find material, it is likely, for many gloomy plays that would turn on the dying away of these old families, and on the lives of the one or two delicate girls that are left so often to represent a dozen hearty men who were alive a generation or two ago. Many of the descendants of these people have, of course, drifted into professional life in Dublin, or have gone abroad; yet, wherever they are, they do not equal their fore-fathers, and where men used to collect fine editions of *Don Quixote* and Molière, in Spanish and French, and luxuriantly bound copies of Juvenal and Persius and Cicero, nothing is read now but Longfellow and Hall Caine and Miss Corelli. Where good and roomy houses were built a hundred years ago, poor and tawdry houses are built now; and bad bookbinding, bad pictures, and bad decorations are thought well of, where rich bindings, beautiful miniatures and finely-carved chimney-pieces were once prized by the old Irish landlords.

J. M. SYNGE, Prose Works

Delville, 6 October 1750 — I am going to make a very comfortable closet: to have a dresser, and all manner of working tools, to keep all my stores for *painting, carving, gilding etc.* for my own room is now so clean and pretty that I cannot suffer it to be strewed with litter, only books and work, and the closet belonging to it to be given up to prints, drawings, and my collection of fossils, petrifactions, and minerals. I have not set them in order yet; a great work it will be, but when done very comfortable. There is to my working closet a pleasant window that over looks all the garden, it faces the east, is always dry and warm. In the middle of the closet a deep nitch with shelves, where I shall put whatever china I think too good for common use, but trifling and insignificant is my *store-room* to what yours is! Mine fits only an idle mind that wants amusement; yours serves either to supply your hospitable table, or gives cordial and healing medicines to the poor and the sick. Your mind is ever turned to help, relieve, and bless your neighbours and acquaintance; whilst mine, I fear (however I may sometimes flatter myself that I have contrary disposition) is *too much filled* with amusement of no real estimation; and when people commend any of my performances I feel a consciousness that my time might have been better employed.

Delville, 5 January 1751 — Family affairs are a necessary evil that must be attended to, and sometimes will break in malapropos. My household at present is in pretty good condition: but I have a great piece of work in hand at present, which is, dusting and airing all the books in the library: for though there is a constant fire there and the room very warm, books contract much moisture, and I have a great pleasure in keeping the library in good order.

Mrs Delaney's Letters

NEW ASCENDENCY

The Protestant newcomers' liveliness and well-being was wholly at the native Catholic expense. The new ascendency lacked feeling: in fact, feeling would have been fatal to it. At the same time, I do honestly think this ascendency identified God with its good luck. The Cromwellian justification was deep in family fibre; innate conviction was at the root of their zest. And, in their three or four generations of life in Ireland, something had worked on their temperaments: they were now Irish in being, if not in interest.

In Queen Anne's reign, anti-popishness in England had been exacerbated by Louis XIV's support of James II's son's claim. During the years of the War of the Spanish Succession it had looked as though the French King might land Prince James Edward in Ireland to raise the Catholics and threaten England's west flank. So, further laws, effectively restrictive and disabling, were passed against Irish Catholics. By the end of Anne's reign, Catholics had been debarred from holding office in the State or army, forbidden to act as grand jurors and finally disenfranchised. Laws forbidding Catholics to inherit land except from each other, to buy more land or to obtain leases of more than thirty-one years stopped any growth (or rather, recovery) of territorial power. A law compelling the estate of any deceased Catholic to be shared out equally between all his sons — unless the eldest 'conformed' before he came of age — aimed at the shredding up of remaining Catholic estates, and at the reduction of Catholic landowning families by bringing them to the small-holder way of life. Catholics were not permitted to carry arms, and, for a short time, as the final humiliation, were not allowed to ride. The same system that denied the Catholic gentry their status pushed the poor right under – they suffered atrociously. The settlers had built their houses out of the stones from ruins; their descendants now built a society out of another ruin.

ELIZABETH BOWEN, *Bowen's Court*

TO RACE, GAMBLE AND DRINK

I was staying the year before the Irish famine at a large house in Connaught. We had a great gathering there of the gentlemen of the county; more than a hundred of us sat down to a luncheon on the lawn. My neighbour at the table was a Scotchman, who was over there examining the capabilities of the soil. 'There,' he said to me, 'you see the landed gentry of this county. In all the number there may be one, at the most two, who believe that the Almighty put them into this world for any purpose but to shoot grouse, race, gamble, drink, or break their necks in the hunting-field. They are not here at all for such purposes, and one day they will find it so.'

The day of reckoning was nearer than he thought. Next year came the potato disease. The estates of most of them were mortgaged, and at best they had only a margin to live upon. Rents could not be paid. The poor people were dying of hunger, and a poor-rate had to be laid on amounting, in places, to confiscation. The Encumbered Estates Act followed, and the whole set of them were swept clean away.

FROUDE, *Short Studies of the Decline of the Landed Gentry*

My hunting began, in late October or early November, with the day when I put on my new habit; and I acknowledge I enjoyed that part of it. How beautifully cut it was, tight about my small waist, the cut-away coat showing the white waistcoat in front! The tying of my stock – from Hodgkinson's – was a dream, but often the stiffened part round my neck cut me horribly. My hat had been made so carefully and was put on so tightly that it was almost impossible to lose it – an important thing if one should fall on one's head – to be sure of that protection! The putting on of my hat was so important that I often did it before I did anything else, and was discovered once by Mrs Jones sitting in my bath with nothing on at all except my top hat over my carefully netted hair. There was not a wrinkle in the legs of my boots. There were none of the soft boots that you see now, in those days. You had to put powder inside them before you could get them on, and they were torture to walk in, or when one was getting on or off a horse. My hair, of course, under my top hat must be irreproachable. If one had appeared in curls in those days as people appear now, one would have looked like a chorus girl, and if I had dared to do such a thing Fingall would have sent me home at once.

But I think I must have done him credit when I emerged dressed for the fray, even if I felt more as if I were dressed for the sacrifice! My heart was always in my boots then, as later. Very pretty boots, fortunately, but still that was no place for my heart to be! I loved meeting my friends, of course, and trotting all together along some bright sunlit road, talking, with the cheerful accompaniment of the horses' hoofs, which no other sound can equal. I have always said that there is no place in the world for getting to know people to be compared to the hunting field. Above all, I think that is true when it is a case of one's future husband or wife. You can see, out hunting, whether a man is selfish or considerate, whether he is a braggart or has courage. And there are so many moments when people can be alone together, easily and naturally, with the country about them, and talk and knowledge of each other come so quickly and are so real in those surroundings. At a covert side waiting, in some moment when the hunt is lost temporarily and two people try together to find it again. (Or, if they are tired of each other, they can always ride away!) And there are the long friendly rides home at the end of the day. There is – I repeat it, as I have often repeated it – no better test of the man you consider as a husband than to spend a day hunting with him.

LADY FINGALL, Memoirs

The hounds were hurried into the fields, the hare was again spurred into action, and I was again confronted with the responsibilities of the chase. After the first five minutes I had discovered several facts about the Quaker. If the bank was above a certain height he refused it irrevocably, if it accorded with his ideas he got his forelegs over and ploughed through the rest of it on his stiflejoints, or, if a gripe made this inexpedient, he remained poised on top till the fabric crumbled under his weight. In the case of walls he butted them down with his knees, or squandered them with his hind legs. These operations took time, and the leaders of the hunt streamed farther and farther away over the crest of a hill, while the Quaker pursued at the equable gallop of a horse in the Bayeux Tapestry.

I began to perceive that I had been adopted as a pioneer by a small band of followers, who, as one of their number candidly explained, 'liked to have someone ahead of them to soften the banks,' and accordingly waited respectfully till the Quaker had made the rough places smooth, and taken the raw edge off the walls. They, in their turn, showed me alternative routes when the obstacle proved above the Quaker's limit; thus, in ignoble confederacy, I and the offscourings of the Curranhilty hunt pursued our way across some four miles of country. When at length we parted it was with extreme regret on both sides. A river crossed our course, with boggy banks pitted deep with the hoof marks of our forerunners; I suggested it to the Quaker, and discovered that Nature had not in vain endued him with the hind quarters of the hippopotamus. I presume the others had jumped it; the Quaker, with abysmal flounder-

ings, walked through and heaved himself to safety on the farther bank. It was the dividing of the ways. My friendly
company turned aside as one man, and I was left with the
world before me, and no guide save the hoof-marks in the
grass. These presently led me to a road, on the other side of
which was a bank, that was at once added to the Quaker's
black list. The rain had again begun to fall heavily, and was
soaking in about my elbows; I suddenly asked myself why, in
heaven's name, I should go any farther. No adequate reason
occurred to me, and I turned in what I believed to be the
direction of Drumcurran.

I rode on for possibly two or three miles without seeing a
human being, until, from the top of a hill I descried a solitary
lady rider. I started in pursuit. The rain kept blurring my eye-
glass, but it seemed to me that the rider was a schoolgirl with
hair hanging down her back, and that her horse was a trifle
lame. I pressed on to ask my way, and discovered that I had
been privileged to overtake no less a person than Miss Bobbie
Bennett.

My question as to the route led to information of a varied
character. Miss Bennett was going that way herself; her mare
had given her what she called 'a toss and a half,' whereby she
had strained her arm and the mare her shoulder, her habit had
been torn, and she had lost all her hairpins.

'I'm an awful object,' she concluded; 'my hair's the plague
of my life out hunting! I declare I wish to goodness I was
bald!'

I struggled to the level of the occasion with an appropriate
protest. She had really very brilliant grey eyes, and her com-
plexion was undeniable. Philippa has since explained to me
that it is a mere male fallacy that any woman can look well
with her hair down her back, but I have always maintained
that Miss Bobbie Bennett, with the rain glistening on her dark
tresses, looked uncommonly well.

'I shall never get it dry for the dance to-night,' she complained.

'I wish I could help you,' said I.

'Perhaps you've got a hairpin or two about you!' said she,
with a glance that had certainly done great execution before
now.

I disclaimed the possession of any such tokens, but volunteered to go and look for some at a neighbouring cottage.

The cottage door was shut, and my knockings were answered by a stupefied-looking elderly man. Conscious of my own absurdity, I asked him if he had any hairpins.

'I didn't see a hare this week!' he responded in a slow bellow.

'Hairpins!' I roared; 'has your wife any hairpins?'

'She has not.' Then, as an afterthought, 'She's dead these ten years.'

At this point a young woman emerged from the cottage, and, with many coy grins, plucked from her own head some half-dozen hairpins, crooked, and grey with age, but still hairpins, and as such well worth my shilling. I returned with my spoil to Miss Bennett, only to be confronted with a fresh difficulty. The arm that she had strained was too stiff to raise to her head.

Miss Bobbie turned her handsome eyes upon me. 'It's no use,' she said plaintively, 'I can't do it!'

I looked up and down the road; there was no one in sight. I offered to do it for her.

Miss Bennett's hair was long, thick, and soft; it was also slippery with rain. I twisted it conscientiously, as if it were a hay rope, until Miss Bennett, with an irrepressible shriek, told me it would break off. I coiled the rope with some success, and proceeded to nail it to her head with the hairpins. At all the most critical points one, if not both, of the horses moved; hairpins were driven home into Miss Bennett's skull, and were with difficulty plucked forth again; in fact, a more harrowing performance can hardly be imagined, but Miss Bennett bore it with the heroism of a pin-cushion.

SOMERVILLE AND ROSS, *Experiences of an Irish RM*

It may perhaps astonish some of my English readers to be told that there were old families holding good positions in their neighbourhoods whose children were never visible except when detected in the act of swinging upon the entrance-gate, or surprised in some out-of-the-way nook in the shrubbery, – the boys with naked knees peeping through their corduroy suits, the girls with battered bonnets and with socks either hanging in wrinkles about their ankles or half-absorbed under the heels of well-worn shoes. When thus caught, the little savages incontinently took to flight.

There were large Country houses within a few miles of us where I never saw any children at all, though I knew there were plenty. In many families the younger branches were invisible, indisputably for economical reasons, but not for this reason alone. The daughters who had been introduced must be considered. To publish the number of those still remaining to be provided for would be the height of imprudence, as the more the children the less the marriage portion, and consequently the smaller the chance of marriage. Such arrangements were much too common for any unfavourable comment to be made.

ANON, *Some Time in Ireland*

It was however true to say that in Ireland grandeur and poverty often walked hand-in-hand. Elizabeth Bowen's life at Bowen's Court inspired those tragic unsurpassed annals of an Irish family before the house met the fate of demolition at the hands of a local farmer. The attitudes of Lady Fingall and Elizabeth Bowen show an awareness of the social and ancestral differences in a country of many racial origins. In their ability to express the subtleties of their class's predicament they were relatively rare. The landowning class were in general incapable or unwilling to admit the uneasiness of their place in Irish life – religion, folk memories and even language underlined the dichotomy of their existence.

DESMOND FITZGERALD, *Vanishing Houses of Ireland*

THE GAP

Charlie's way with the men and women who worked for him was casual and friendly, without the forced intimacy or superior tone used by many of his class, and without religious prejudice. I was the only Protestant among them, my father and uncle like his had been Indian army officers, but his manner to me was the same as his manner to them, which pleased me. Ivy, whose warm-heartedness expressed itself more openly than his, was set apart from them – painfully for her because she had a loving curiosity and concern for other people that drew them towards her. Her kind actions were far more frequent than his. If someone was ill or had a roof that leaked, he might not notice though he spoke to most of them or rode past their houses every day. (His own roof leaked, of course, and he was never ill.) But she would do something about it at once.

Betrothals, marriages and births were single occasions for him on which he behaved with extravagant generosity, making the neighbouring landowners laugh at him a bit, but for her they were also the beginning of new lives which she kept close to for years. So naturally she was loved. But because of the religion of the people who loved her she could not wholly return their love. She could not trust them. Doubt spoils love. She said to me more than once that Roman Catholic teaching was founded on deceit; for example that the high-ups of that Church thought of trans-substantiation as symbolically true, but taught it as though it were literally true. She believed that anyone brought up in an atmosphere of deceit must acquire a deceitful nature. It was impossible to trust a Roman Catholic. She distrusted those of her own class, especially doctors, and never thought as I did that she had merely found for herself a reason to explain the gap she so much wished to close between her ways and those of the people of Woodbrook.

I don't think the Kirkwoods knew much about the horrid legacy we had all inherited. English school books, or at least the ones I read as a boy, glossed over the atrocities of the Penal Laws or at best described them as over and done with, like the rack and thumbscrew, curiosities of a barbarous age. But the sins of the fathers can never be over and done with. The deceit-fulness which Ivy saw in the Irish was a form of defence adopted by their fathers against one of the most brutal systems of oppression in the history of mankind, a defence that had become unnecessary and unconscious. I don't mean that the early Christians, the Huguenots, the Swedish Catholics, the witches, or the Jewish and gipsy peoples of my own time suffered less, but in most other religious persecutions I have read of the oppressors were in the majority. A long-lasting system was not needed, so the bout of sadism died out and though it might be succeeded by another its memory would be diffused among the scattered victims.

DAVID THOMSON, *Woodbrook*

In the eighteenth century young people of quality were not sent to schools, nor was a general governess or tutor 'of all work' kept. Tutor specialists went from house to house; one time it was the writing master, next a French *émigré* or a Latin-learned parson, a dancing-mistress succeeded to a person who had dealt with more serious branches of culture, and the wandering minstrel was detained on his journey as a guest in some great house to give sets of harp-lessons to the family and neighbours.

Sydney Owenson gives a description of her own *début* as a governess, which contrasts delightfully with the dismal experiences of Charlotte Brontë. Leaving a dance in Dublin attired in muslin and pink silk stockings, with no time to change, she bundled herself up in a great Irish cloak, and went by coach to the country house of a Mrs Fetherston-haugh in West-meath. The dinner party on her arrival included the lady of the house, her two daughters, two itinerant preceptors, Mr O'Hanlon, a writing and elocution-master, and a dancing-master, Father Murphy, the P.P., and the Rev. Mr Beaufort, Protestant curate.

The parish priest proposed the health of the new governess, and after dinner the butler announced 'that the piper had come from Castletown to play in Miss Owenson, upon which the girls immediately proposed a dance in the back hall, and when I told them I was a famous jig-dancer they were perfectly enraptured. So we set to, all the servants crowding round the two open doors in the hall.'

CHARLOTTE MULLIGAN FOX, *Annals of the Irish Harpers*

My mother and I first started gun-slinging, as it were, in 1922. The Irish Civil War was in progress and one of its victims – or very likely to be if he didn't look slippy – was my father, then a member of the Cosgrave Government. He had returned once to our house outside Dublin with three perceptible bullet holes in the back door of his car, in no mood to share my mother's opinion, aimed at restoring his confidence, that the IRA had probably mistaken him for someone else. The shots had, apparently, been fired near Portobello Bridge. So sure was my father of their intended destination that he covered the three miles home in three minutes, and went straight to bed.

When, therefore, the thunderous banging came on the back door a few nights later it had the effect of freezing him to his armchair, in which he'd been reading the evening paper. It was my mother who went to the top of the kitchen stairs, to see what was afoot. I joined her almost immediately, a pale lad of nine, having been roused from my sleep by the noise. I'd been sleeping badly of recent weeks because it was nearly Christmas, and my whole soul was crying out to take possession of my first Hornby train.

'It's all right,' my mother said, taking her customarily steady view, 'it's only some men.'

We heard the bolts being shot on the back door, and then the voice of the cook raised in indignant surprise. She was a loyal retainer, who'd been with the family for some years. 'It's youse lot, is it?' she said. 'Janey, I thought yez wasn't comin' till half-eleven.' It was, in fact, only ten-fifteen.

A male voice said peevishly, 'Ah, don't be shoutin' . . .' and then the first of the raiders came running up the stairs. I had a brief glimpse of a gun, then a face masked with a cap and a handkerchief. My mother stopped him dead. 'If there's going to be any murder,' she said, 'you can get back out of that and go home.'

More masked faces and caps appeared at the bottom of the stairs. Querulous voices arose. 'What's the matter, Mick?' 'Get on with it, can't ya?' But Mick was explaining the matter to my mother.

'Nobody's gettin' shot, mum. You needn't take on. We've

orders to burn down the house, that's all.' He sounded injured by the false impression.

'You're sure of that?' my mother asked him, wishing to have the matter absolutely clear for the benefit of my father, in the event that he was still able to receive messages, in the next room.

'There'll be nobody shot,' said another raider impatiently. 'Now will you stand back owa that an' let's get on with it. We haven't all night.'

My mother remained firm. With the first matter on the agenda settled to her satisfaction, she passed to others, now of equal importance. 'What about all my lovely books?' she said. 'First editions, signed by Lawrence and Katherine Mansfield and Middleton Murry. And the pictures – Orpens, Gertlers, the little drawings by John . . .'

The raiders, jammed on the stairs, were getting hot and angry. An exposed youth, still stuck in the passage, was being berated by the cook. He appeared to be a cousin of hers, and was refusing to carry her trunk out into the garden.

'All right, all *right* . . .' said the first raider. The protracted conversation was causing the handkerchief to slip off his face. 'Take out anything you want, but for God's love hurry up about it.' He turned to the men behind. 'Who's got the pethrol an' the matches?' he wanted to know.

At this point my father appeared in the hall, unobtrusively, and still unsure of his welcome. The raiders appealed to him. 'Ask your missus to give us a chance, sir, will ya? Sure, we're only actin' under ordhers . . .'

He took command, in a voice slightly higher than normal, advising me to wake my sister, still peacefully asleep, and to put on some warm clothes. He then suggested to my mother that they should both try to save a few personal mementoes before we all withdrew to safety in the garden.

'And leave,' my mother cried passionately, 'all the children's Christmas toys behind? Certainly not!'

The possible outcome of the night struck home to me for the first time. 'Me train!' I cried. 'Don't let them burn me train!'

PATRICK CAMPBELL, *South of the Border*

Galway is a rich place. In the evenings, at the best hotel, the survivors of the old upper-class life turn up – remarkably dressed women of a certain age, horsy, sporting, excitable in the Irish fashion. There is an easygoing dash in their appearance, and a marked eccentricity if one compares them with their more stolid opposite numbers in Cheltenham or Bath, knitting or sleeping over their novels. There is a touch of outrageous gaiety. You hear flattering phrases – the first duty of man and woman is to charm, and to hell with the rest.

V. S. PRITCHETT, *At Home and Abroad*

LISNABRIN, CURRAGLASS

A five-bay bow-ended house with a Diocletian window above a Venetian doorway. The seat of the Crokers, descended from a Cromwellian Colonel to whom the estate was granted. By a happy coincidence, Col Croker had been given shelter at Lisnabrin by its Irish Catholic owner, Walter Coppinger, and nursed back to health by his two daughters, having been brought here gravely wounded in a battle nearby. So instead of turning Coppinger out, Croker asked him for the hand of one of his daughters, and became his son-in-law.

MARK BENCE JONES, *Guide to Irish Country Houses*

MOUNT IVERS

Sixmilebridge is a nice eighteenth-century village intended for a prosperous future it never attained, and it contains one of the most beautiful of Irish houses of Queen Anne date, Mount Ivers. This is a very tall house, more like a tower than a house, with tall steps, tall, narrow doorways and tall windows, all with the original heavy sashes. It replaced a fortified house, of which the main chimney-piece is in the hall, and it contains a number of fine mantelpieces by Bossi. There is also a painting of the house as it was intended to be and never became, with gardens like those of a French château. A tall house with tall notions, for you have only to mount the stairs to see where the money gave out on the first landing, and the windows are still unpanelled, and in the attics you can see the plaster centre-pieces all ready to be fixed up, and can visualise that sad morning when carpenters and plasterers realised that they would never be paid and set off on the journey back to Limerick.

FRANK O'CONNOR, *Munster, Leinster and Connaught*

... Meanwhile the Gaelic culture ran underground, with its ceaseless poetry of lament. (Gaelic was spoken in the kitchens and fields and in untouched country the settlers did not know.) It has taken the decline of the Anglo-Irish to open to them the poetry of regret: only dispossessed people know their land in the dark.

ELIZABETH BOWEN, *Bowen's Court*

ACKNOWLEDGEMENTS

We would like to thank Donald Brady and his staff at Lismore Library for patient and generous assistance, also Cork City Reference Library, and Mrs Phyllis Mitchell, Nicholas Burke and the Knight of Glin for kindly giving us the run of their private libraries and for their illuminating suggestions.

We deeply appreciate the many friends who helped us with ideas and quotations, in particular, Gina Pollinger, Catherine Stroud, Richard Walsh of Lismore Library, Sean Dunne, Thomas McCarthy, Paddy Rossmore, Tony Gallagher, Hurd Hatfield, Alexander Cockburn, Gerald McSweeney, Ken and Rachel Thompson, Rosemary FitzGerald, Denis FitzGerald, George Phipps, Richard Wood.

We also owe thanks to Myrtle Allen for her kindness in allowing us to use the office machinery at Ballymaloe House and to Natacha Harty for her unfailing help.

We are grateful to the following authors, owners of copyright, publishers and literary agents who have kindly given permission for poems and passages of prose to appear in this anthology.

Anvil Press and Thomas McCarthy for 'Doreen! Doreen!' from *The Sorrow Garden* by Thomas McCarthy; Atlantic Monthly Press for extracts from Sean O'Faolain's *Vive Moi*; Barrie & Jenkins for extracts from *Woodbrook* by David Thomson; Blood-axe Books for Brendan Kennelly's 'Light Dying' from *A Time for Voices*; John Calder and the Estate of Samuel Beckett for extracts from *The Expelled* and *First Love* by Samuel Beckett; Carcanet Press for Eavan Boland's 'After a Childhood Away From Ireland' from *Outside History*; Chatto & Windus for extracts from V.S. Pritchett's *At Home and Abroad* and Maurice O'Sullivan's *Twenty Years A-Growing*; Constable and Company for an extract from *Guide to Irish Country Houses* by Mark

Bence-Jones; Curtis Brown for extracts from *The Year of Liberty* by Thomas Pakenham, from *Bowen's Court* by Elizabeth Bowen; John F. Deane of Dedalus Press for poems from Thomas Kinsella's *Poems of the Dispossessed*; J.M. Dent & Sons for extracts from *Lovely is the Lee* by Robert Gibbings, and *Experiences of an Irish RM* by Somerville and Ross; The Gallery Press for John Montague's 'Windharp' from *New Selected Poems*, Medbh McGuckian's 'Gateposts' from *Marconi's Cottage*; Sean Dunne and the Gallery Press for poems from *The Sheltered Nest* by Sean Dunne; Faber & Faber Limited for poems from *Selected Poems* by Seamus Heaney, *Translations* by Brian Friel, *Collected Poems* by Louis MacNeice, *High Island* by Richard Murphy; and extracts from *Preoccupations* by Seamus Heaney and *Midway on the Waves* by James Lees Milne; Gill & Macmillan Limited for extracts from *Hidden Ireland* by Daniel Corkery; the author and Gill & Macmillan for extracts from *Ballymaloe Cookbook* by Myrtle Allen; Gollancz for extracts from *Everything to Lose* by Frances Partridge, and *The Face and Mind of Ireland* by Arland Ussher; Elaine Greene Ltd for extracts from *States of Ireland* by Conor Cruise O'Brien; Hamish Hamilton for extracts from *A Talent to Annoy* by Nancy Mitford, *The Great Hunger* by Cecil Woodham-Smith; the author and Hamish Hamilton for an extract from *Black Baby* by Clare Boylan; HarperCollinsPublishers for extracts from *Memoirs* by Lady Fingall, *The Third Policeman* by Flann O'Brien, Ulick O'Connor's *Oliver St John Gogarty: A Poet and His Times*; and for 'The Pleasure Ground' by Richard Murphy taken from *An Irish Childhood* ed. A. Norman Jeffares and Antony Kamm; David Higham Associates for an extract from *Dublin Phoenix* by Olivia Robertson; Hoggis & Figgis for extracts from Praegar's *The Way That I Went* and Nora Robertson's *The Crowned Harp*, and for poems from Douglas Hyde's *Studies and Translations from the Irish*; Mrs Irene Josephy and the Estate of Patrick Campbell for extracts from *35 Years on the Job* and *South of the Border* by Patrick Campbell; Lilliput Press for extracts from George O'Brien's *The Village of Longing*, Hubert Butler's *Escape from the Anthill*, George Moore's *Hail and Farewell*; Little, Brown and Company for an extract from *The Noels and the Milbankes*, edited by Mark Edwin; Longmans Green for an extract from *The Letters of Countess de Markievicz* ed. Esther Roper; Robert B. Luce Inc. for an extract from Honor Tracy's *Mind You, I've Said Nothing!*; Macmillan Limited for extracts from Conrad Arensberg's *The Irish Countryman*, Frank O'Connor's *Irish Poetry AD 600–1200*, Sean O'Casey's *Innisfallen Fare Thee Well*; Macmillan Inc. for extracts from AE's *The Living Torch*; Mercier Press for extracts from Mary Carberry's *The Farm by Lough Gur*, Conchur O Siochain's *The Man from Cape Clear*, *The Field* by John B. Keane, *The Diary of Humphrey O'Sullivan* trans. by Thomas de Bhaldraith, *Book of Irish Curses* by Patrick C. Parer, Martin Brian O'Keefe for extracts from *Tarry Flynn* by Patrick Kavanagh; Methuen Limited for extracts from H.V. Morton's *In Search of Ireland*; John Murray for extracts and poems from Dervla Murphy's *Wheels Within Wheels*, John Betjeman's *Collected Poems*, *The Batchelor Duke* by James Lees Milne; John O'Meara for extracts from Giraldis Cambrensis's *History and Topography of Ireland*, translated by John O'Meara; Oxford University Press for extracts and poems from Tomas O'Crohan's *The Island Man* (trans. Robin Flower), and a poem from *The Western Island* by Robin Flower; Penguin Books Limited for extracts from *Home Before Night* by Hugh Leonard; Peters, Fraser & Dunlop for extracts from *Leinster, Munster & Connaught* by Frank O'Connor and *Beyond the Pale* by William Trevor; Random House Inc. for extract from *Annagh Keen* by Deborah Love; Raven Arts Press for the poem by Nuala Ni Dhomhnaill from *Selected Poems*; Tessa Sayle Agency and Alexander Cockburn for extracts from *I, Claud* by Claud Cockburn; Sheil Land Associates for extracts from *Cappaghglass* by Peter Somerville-Large; The Society of Authors and James Stephens estate for a poem, and extracts from *Irish Fairy Tales*; Abner Stein Ltd for an extract from Denis Johnston's *The Old Lady Says 'No'*; Thames & Hudson for an extract from Michael MacLiammor's *Ireland*; Verso and Alexander Cockburn for extracts from *Corruptions of Empire* by Alexander Cockburn; Viking for an extract from *The Railway Station Man* by Jennifer Johnstone; Woolfhound Press for their translation of Alexis de Toqueville's *Journey in Ireland*; Weidenfeld & Nicolson for extracts from Edna O'Brien's *A Pagan Place*, and *Evelyn Waugh, Letters*, edited by Mark Amory.

Every effort has been made to contact the copyright owners of material included in this anthology. In the instances where this has not proved possible, we offer our apologies to those concerned.

INDEX